Talking
with
strangers

Open up to strangers you may meet
Inquire authentically about their lives
Avoid judgement and preconceptions
And you will start to connect to others
You will join a kind of human web
And encounter unexpected synchronicities

Neil Moffatt

With special thanks to :

Robert Lombardo PhD for urging me to write the book

Talia Stimpson for support and encouragement

First edition January 2020

Cover image courtesy of https://www.goodfreephotos.com

Watercolour conversions of photographs I took on my travels have been converted by the wonderful **Waterlogue** program.

Why talk with strangers?

Here in Britain, we tend to teach our children not to talk to strangers. It aligns with the British culture, which also asks us to speak only when spoken to first. Quite how that is supposed to work, who knows. Maybe that is why we often struggle to talk with strangers beyond a simple 'hello, how are you?' We also tend to forget to tell children when they grow up that it is now OK to talk with strangers.

Part of the problem is that we use a judgemental word to describe people we do not know. They are, somehow, *strange*. We do not mean that when we refer to *strangers*, but the implication still permeates the meaning. Better to see that they are *new, unknown* people rather than strange. And maybe also *knowable* by implication. The words we choose carry much greater weight than we often realise.

Besides, even when growing up, every person we meet is essentially a stranger the very first time we encounter them, even if a family member. And it may well be the case that some aunts, uncles and grandparents are harder for children to relate to than the strangers they meet – the new children they learn to play with in parks or in school for example.

Historically, fear of strangers has deep roots in our genetic past. Close-knit tribal communities tended to treat those of other tribes with hostility. A stranger was someone generally to be feared (or mated with). Unlike most animals, however, humans have evolved to intermingle with strangers on a daily basis in towns and cities. We generally underestimate how much of an achievement it has been to now coexist calmly and peaceably with hundreds and thousands of strangers around us, even though being able to is vital to the fluid functioning of urban life. However, it is not always harmonious, with misconstrued looks leading to conflict for example, and alcohol readily and frequently undermining the delicate foundation of

1

our tolerance of the difference and unfamiliarity of others. But we Brits are, nevertheless, mostly very accommodating of strangers, even if all too often in a stand-off manner.

Sadly, however, in the US and increasingly in Britain, a Darwinian 'survival of the fittest' individualism is being promoted by governments. This can and does undermine our social fabric and can regress us to hold more primitive fears of strangers. Or simply a fear of 'others'.

Yet business thrives on the synergy of the collective – of people working for a common good. The many are indeed often greater than the sum of their number. In society also, where meeting places such as coffee shops, pubs, theatres and shopping centres often act as social lubricants. They connect people and nourish those connections.

But we connect with strangers more readily when we are receptive to them. When we put our own agenda behind that of others, we are in a better position to talk with strangers. When we show genuine interest in the unknown, but knowable life of each new person we meet, we grow spiritually.

Sometimes, it is no more than a few exchanged words.

Sometimes, it can lead to a sustained conversation.

Sometimes it can lead to a friendship.

The more that we explore and embrace connections with others, the more we enter the web of human relations. The atoms we are composed of are themselves parts of great webs – likewise the cells in our body. This connectivity and interaction is one of the underlying themes of the Universe.

To connect with others is a kind of calling.

By contrast, when we disconnect, we can become isolated, where the absence of a feeling of being a part of a web of people can see us atrophy and fade away, in effect as a result of being denied meaning from others.

If you think that talking with strangers is a matter for extrovert, bullish, outward going people, then you are wrong! It may take time for shy and introverted types to connect with others, but repeated, simple hellos and brief exchanges will reveal the reality that *most people most of the time are nice* and most are happy to chat even if initially only about themselves. Listen to them and they will often be receptive and open out to you. So a fear of talking with strangers is often quite unfounded.

2

$\mathcal{A}$ Sociable introvert

I am a social introvert, born in London in the year 1957.

This is a story of my talks with strangers that I met during 2019.

Many people simplistically presume that introverts always prefer to hide in books and avoid contact with others and that extroverts have the monopoly on sociability. But social natures are rarely as fully polarised as this, and are more often shades of grey rather than absolutes.

At root, introverts tend to get their energy from thinking, being creative, reading and watching, while extroverts need the company of others as a kind of energising fuel. Introverts get easily overloaded, while extroverts needs lots of stimulation.

Neither is 'correct'.

They are just different, but, sadly, people often fail to understand or reconcile these different ways of being.

You might be surprised to learn that introverts can actually be more sociable than extroverts. Their keener sensitivities enable them to tune in better to others, to be more interested in what others say and how they live their lives. But they can only socialise for so long before they get overloaded, burnt out, and need hours to recharge away from the company if people. This is how I am.

3

But introversion does not define who I am, of course. It is one factor only. I am also hyper-sensitive at times, my over-reactions to even trivial events becoming seismic in scale. A series of relatively traumatic events a few decades coupled with my hyper-sensitivity to burden me with decades of tension headaches, bouts of anxiety, depression and panic attacks. A toxic cocktail. I might feel uniquely unfairly mistreated by life, but countless others suffer similarly and countless others endure far worse. More brutal, by far, are cluster headaches, where the pain is so intense that sufferers can resort to banging their head against the wall to try to alleviate the pain.

A key trigger for my tension headaches is social anxiety. Certain social situations are triggers, such as being trapped with someone devoid of empathy who regales endless stories with no care as to whether I am listening or indeed interested. This is not dialogue but monologue.

So why should I, of all people, actually go out of my way to talk with strangers? This is a pertinent question of course. Greeting new people I meet has actually been a long standing hobby of mine, even though it can trigger headaches that last the rest of the day – I can and do meet people that I really wish I had not spoken to.

So why this hobby for an introvert afflicted with social anxiety?

To understand, you probably need to have a personal experience of adversity of similar magnitude and enduring nature. It creates a strong desire to be released from the pull of the *gravity* of these conditions; to rise above the quagmire. Deep engagement in exciting conversation provides a magnificent escape from my blighted plight and the endless self-focus that it generates. If just occasionally it backfires and triggers more headaches or anxiety, then so be it. The chance of escape is generally worth the risk.

Because I get excited by new encounters (along with repeat encounters, I should add), the recipient of my often jolly chat feels this and tends to get energised by it also. A virtuous feedback loop can thereby grow.

When I meet someone new I tend to ask, with genuine interest, about themselves. Their profession, interests and nature. In general, people like to talk about themselves. And I often find it akin to opening a new book – each person I encounter is necessarily unique and different.

Meeting and talking with many new people also serves to quash the habit of judging people by their appearance because you start to see a pattern of visual, superficial judgement dispelled by the true nature exuding

4

from within. Additionally, you start to see and separate cultural effects in someone you meet from their own uniqueness. We are all a mix of conditioned and individualistic natures and it can be fascinating to see where culture stops and individuality steps in.

I talk at bus stops, in coffee shops, supermarket queues, even walking along the street. I actually met my wife-to-be in a chat group at the back of the bus to work when I lived in Portsmouth.

The hundreds of books, mostly non-fiction, that I have read enables me to talk about many subjects. This allows me to connect to many others – to share in their domains of expertise, at least a little. And the Eastern philosophy I have read and absorbed (in principle if not always in practice) allows me to treat each new person with minimal or zero judgement. I keep working at this as there are many parts of the subconscious that are operating when we are in dialogue with others that can undermine such ideologies.

I try to accept any such part of my mind that tries to compromise my treatment of others. That I should have such derailing urges does not negate or devalue my approach as I do not consciously choose them. I merely strive to starve them of the oxygen of attention they need to survive. My intended unconditional acceptance of each person I meet seems generally to be felt and reflected by them. When they sense that I will not judge them they generally relax and feel assured that they can open out safely with me.

During the writing of this book, I was asked a number of very good questions by **Talia**, who you will meet shortly, that I will now try to answer.

1. How did I start to talk with strangers?

My instinct was to say that it was a recent thing, that started a few years ago, when watching football games in the pub where I learnt to engage in conversation with others also watching. It was often hard to connect, as many just wanted to watch the match. And it was especially hard with those supporting the other team, who generally tend to feel obliged to act out the aggressive adversary role. But I worked away at this task, made easier when I encountered someone I had sat with on another occasion, where familiarity can soften relationships. My overall aim was to enhance the football watching with shared chat and joy or angst depending on the action on the screen.

But I reflected further and realised that I connected with others socially and at work when much younger. Certainly in my late twenties, I talked with the group of people in the opened seating area at the back of the bus to work. Seats at the back and the sides faced the centre aisle. I became a kind of cohesive social force that connected together the dozen or so people in this part of the bus.

Even then, there was a sense of challenge, with ages ranging from school children to the elderly. I guess it was natural for me to do this uniting thing and also to want to do it. To connect, to create a warm, welcoming, inclusive environment. In work, likewise, I would often be found chatting away as much as working.

It is is salient to note that going further back, especially in my teens, I was particularly shy, especially so with strangers. People can and do change.

2. What was the tipping point?

I cannot recall a time where I transitioned from reserved to being comfortable with strangers. I can only presume it was an incremental process with steps forward as well as backward.

3. Is it natural for me to talk with strangers?

To a very large degree, it feels quite natural to do so. But I think my original shyness shows that it was actually an acquired ability. I have always had the pressure of speech and curiosity of mind as latent, foundational skills. When I additionally built up a large and diverse mental library of things to say, and comments to offer on the activities of others, these skills were able to start flourishing or manifesting.

Maybe surprisingly, I genuinely struggle to see my comfort and flexibility talking with complete strangers as a skill. I feel more that it is an iteratively acquired capability. Just as language itself. And that it is something I generally enjoy talking with strangers so much that I want to nourish and hone the ability.

So it is undoubtably largely the sheer repetition of practice that makes it become or appear natural. I am strongly motivated where others might be deterred by a few early difficulties. My seemingly insatiable desire to understand and connect with others allows me to treat difficulties not as impediments but as opportunities to learn and refine my interaction abilities.

Having inherited a near-polymath nature, comfortable in the arts as

6

much as with technology and science, I can see from many different viewpoints. It allows me to empathise with creatives as well as analytical people. This multi-dimensional nature also extends to the age of people I meet. I can be childish and child-like with the young and serious and adult-like with adults. At least mostly – some people I necessarily am not able to connect with.

One friend last century described me as a chameleon, changing depending on who I am with. She saw that this kind of made me less authentic – she was pretty invariant in nature so you can understand that viewpoint.

4. What have I learnt?

A great deal, but it is not so easy to quantify. And I actually do not want to quantify what is essentially a qualitative thing. But in summary, I add to my knowledge about the world from conversations, and about human nature, and revel in the exquisite dance that is conversation between human beings. Talking is, incidentally, one of the most thorough of exercises for the brain, concurrently using many different regions. The process of leaving oneself and enquiring into the life and the present moment of someone else has proven to be a fantastic antidote to the isolation of living alone with mental health problems.

Escaping from the gravity of my plight into the lives of others is matched only by engagement in social sports – during a game of football, for example, I feel that I become part of the team, and less an individual. And with sport as with chatting with strangers, I can readily forget that I am feeling poorly, even if there are occasions where the act of conversation can readily tire me and also exacerbate poor health symptoms. The contrast with, and counter-point to, the hours spent hibernating away nursing a poorly head are immense, making engagement with others so often thrilling.

Even when the conversation is simple and uneventful.

The value in being connected with others – to be part of the human web – is a vital lesson that I learnt and feel most tangibly in my travels.

5. What has challenged me along the way?

One great challenge is certainly how to handle certain, difficult people. Some are negative and others very draining, egocentric to their core. Some confront me about my beliefs and only until very recently did I overcome the instinct to take umbrage at these perceived 'attacks'. So the maturation of the process of learning about others and of adapting fast to avoid too much negativity from those I met, and too much negativity in my reactivity took quite some time, but has been deeply valuable and welcome.

I also had to tame my instincts to get irritable at the things some people say! People can often pay only scant attention to what we say and thereby ask the silliest of questions that a moment of attention and thought would have avoided. I essentially do not 'take kindly to fools' but work very hard at being more tolerant in this regard.

I also get irritated by loud voices and other noises (more about this later). I guess by the time you are sixty two, emotions tend to ease back, and reactivity is less of a beast to tame. The consequence is that what was originally seen as challenging is now seen in a very different light. I tend to embrace whatever I perceive, whether familiar to myself or alien. And that then makes it easier for me to be wide open to others. The Buddhist concepts I mentioned help enormously in this regard. On reflection, when I am talking with a new stranger and feel no pull of judgement about them, the liberating feeling this gives is beyond words. A freedom that feels so pure, emancipating and quite delicious so it rarely feels like a challenge.

6. Why do doubts not hold me back?

A good question.

Since I have absolutely no idea about each of the many strangers I meet, and I open out to them as fully as possible, then I leave myself wide open, so I probably should harbour some doubts as to the consequences. I could be defensive about my religious (atheist) position, or defensive about my mental health issues, or my aged appearance. Or to be terribly afraid of saying the wrong thing – of upsetting others. But the very act of being as open and authentic as I can seems to placate such fears. Because I aim to hide nothing, except where it might hurt or offend another, then I feel I can handle attacks. I have been endowed with a pretty able and agile mind, so that helps. The training in acceptance and non-judgement along with being fortunate at having a pretty robust self-esteem helps. It allows me to be entirely happy to admit my failings with no or little impact on my sense of self. I accept them as much as I do in others (but I do still try to work on them).

7. How do my conversations affect how I see humanity?

One of the fascinations talking with **Talia** are such questions, and this is an extremely insightful inquiry. (She will read these words and I repeat to her that I do not say them for effect – this is the genuine way I perceive her). For starters, I will quote a telling line from a book I read a while ago :

Most people most of the time across the world are nice

It is worth reflecting on that. The more that I open out to people I chance to encounter, the more this rings true. That it is so life-affirming to chat with what seems to be an endless stream of friendly people makes this unusual hobby more and more beguiling. I am drawn repeatedly to talk with people wherever I go. Even in the lift where there is an unwritten British obligation that all occupants must remain stiff lipped and feel slightly scared and uneasy, (and Heaven forbid that anyone should fart!) Breaking down the barriers that separate us, disarming people in all walks of life creates a warm, wonderful feeling. No longer am I an outsider, but I am now on the *inside* of the human web. I am an active catalyst, embracing others and linking into their lives, even if only very briefly. And this can soften the British reserve, to show, by example to others that we can connect wherever we meet people.

Some encounters in the near past

Before I proceed with stories of people I met in 2019, I offer some tales from a while earlier, starting with a chance encounter with an Indian man at the seating outside Coffee #1 in Penarth (near Cardiff). This exemplifies what started happening as a result of the acceptance approach I described earlier.

This painfully thin man abruptly asked me if he could sit at my table. My instinctive reaction was negatively defensive in large part because there was no chair at my table he could actually sit on. My mind operated in a simple fashion, logically, that no chair meant no one could ask to sit. I hate that stupid simplicity of my mind, but learn to bypass its urges.

Fortunately, I did indeed allow this feeling to fade away. I regrouped my mind and said it was of course fine for him to sit. He grabbed a chair, sat down, and the two of us embarked on the most extraordinary conversational journey. Alas, my poor memory can recount very little, except that we connected in a way that I had never experienced with any human before, and have not done since, and suspect never will again. Here was the most searingly honest, delightful person, humble but simultaneously enlightened as you might ever be lucky to meet in one life time.

It created such an amazing feeling inside that I could be so connected to such a special person that it clearly affected him also. His spirit was not quashed by the terminal cancer he was harbouring. It made me feel rather humble that someone suffering not only with this but also pretty severe spine curvature should be so warm and open to a complete stranger.

About half an hour later, he thanked me for chatting. I gave him my card and hoped to see him again or hear from him. Alas, I did not hear from him or see him again. So far. I do not judge that he did not contact me as I do not know why. But to meet him again would probably tarnish the memory I have, even though that memory is spartan in details.

On another occasion a few years ago, I sat next to a lady on a bus back home to Cardiff. She was happy to chat, and very jolly and engaging she was. Her home was in Penarth but she just happened this day to be travelling in my town. Maybe to enliven the chat, I talked about tennis and she asked if I played at the Mackintosh Tennis Club. This is indeed my tennis club, conveniently located at the end of my road. She said her husband used to play there before they moved to Penarth. Suddenly, she asked if I was Neil because her husband mentioned that name a lot. Yes, I replied, and it dawned on me that her husband must be **Kofe** – the player I clashed most with at the tennis club because he was so very quiet and unsociable, who frequently complained that I talked too much, as indeed I often do. But his wife was as chatty as myself, so it puzzled me how he might cope with her when he could not with me. Maybe she spoke more sense.

There came a point when more of these strange 'coincidences' or connections manifested in my encounters. I regaled some of them to **Thomas Lombardo**, an American author I occasionally communicate with by email. It was his suggestion that I write the stories into a book. It felt indulgent to do so, but not long after starting, it felt cathartic to write and seemed to be a catalyst for more encounters.

Before I go any further, I must categorically state with absolute firmness that the tales recounted here are authentic and genuine. They may sound contrived, but they are recounted faithfully as I experienced them.

I scoured my Social Media history to unearth some early meetings with strangers. Then I started to write up each incident within a day or so of them happening, so my poor memory was not an issue. I hope that these stories encourage you to engage with people you meet wherever you go.

JAN 3 In the gym

One of the people I have met at the gym I attend is very chirpy, frequently and easily animated in both speech and gesture. It is clear, however, that he has some sort of impediment as his speech is rather slurred and repetitive. But his heart is good, he is naturally funny, and I like to treat him with equanimity. Today he asked my name.

After I told him, I asked "And your name?"

He replied "Yes".

So I thought he had not understood.

But he had understood, because his name is "Naim".

JAN 13 Talking with many people

A surreal morning, blighted by anxiety, but filled in abundance with connections to others as if my anxiety was utterly invisible. I had decided to try to escape from this cloying affliction by chatting with the two families I often sit with on Sunday mornings in Coffee #1 in Wellfield Road, five minutes walk from my house in Cardiff. Their two and five year old children sat with me. When they left, another five year old child sat near to me while waiting for his father to be served at the counter. This boy was quite forward, declaring great skill at maths. That made the lady to the left of me giggle. I subsequently talked with an Everton Football Club supporter who was remarkably well informed about my team Liverpool.

Another lady, **Lynne**, then asked to sit near me, and we had a nice chat. I gave her a copy of "Think More", the book I released to Amazon at the start of this year. (The full title is "A clarion call in just 100 pages to urge you to Think More"). I also gave a copy to **Ed** who was reading a George Monbiot book on the environment when I popped upstairs to exercise my sore knees. He is an ecologist I met a while back, who is clearly motivated to help save endangered species.

I then took the bus to Waitrose in Pontprennau, a journey through some of the plentiful Cardiff greenery. I found myself chatting with a five year old and his mother on the bus. My anxiety at this stage was much reduced, the transference of focus from self to others allowing such affliction to fade in potency. Alas, I spoke with a very intense man on the same bus who felt it

11

appropriate to regale me with the story of his migration from 'fags' to 'vapes'. The inherent risk in talking with strangers is that sometimes you regret very swiftly doing so. Fortunately, it rarely happens.

Waitrose is a co-operative store, where profits are shared amongst the staff. A kind of oasis in a desert of vulture businesses who channel profits to a few and remote rich owners and shareholders. I got my customary free cup of tea, a perk for being a card-bearing customer, and chatted for about forty-five minutes with a mix of customers. One man in particular was very well informed. He was a "Spectator" reader, therefore likely to be right wing, and far removed from my left-wing position. Yet we managed to navigate our conversation via a fair bit of common ground.

Another man I talked with spoke just like the "Private Eye" editor Ian Hislop, yet was an accountant by profession. A very entertaining fellow! The final person I chatted with was an elderly lady who mentioned how cold her hands were. And they really were chilly as was most apparent when my hot mitts embraced them. This is a connection at a more intimate level – a kind of special cementing of connection. She declared that she could not remember when her hands were last held by another. Such words I find so wonderfully endearing.

During the near three hours of these meetings, my anxiety ebbed and flowed, but I did not incur a tension headache, which is quite surprising. It would seem that when my mind has thrown me the anxiety curved ball, it sees little reason to also inflict the dead-eye headache ball.

FEB 4 The Japanese lady

The bench high at the top of the Cardiff Castle grounds is one of my favourite places to sit. Atop a tall grassy slope, it looks down over the splendid castle and grounds along with the skyline of the compact city centre. I frequently sit to read but also to relax and gaze out across the vista in front of me. It is an especially great place to talk with strangers as the visitors come from across the world.

Today, a Japanese lady stopped to talk with me. Her name was **Nana** and she had the most enchanting smile and delightfully disarming demeanour. At odds with Japanese cultural norms, she declared that she was comfortable talking to strangers. And, maybe more unusually, she was authentically open in her manner. This was not a presentation of guarded 'niceties' that is often how I perceive Japanese visitors, even though I have a soft spot for these people.

She drew me under her spell, like a siren, and I soon found myself walking down the steps to base level and towards the castle grounds entrance with her. As we chatted, it occurred to me that I had never met a stranger so delightfully warm, open and friendly. Not ever. She made me feel relaxed and to wish to spend the rest of the day with her. And she hinted that she also wished the same. I guess she was in her 20's or 30's so this is unusual. Frustratingly, however, I was getting hungry and wanted to avoid the headaches that can result from delayed meals. So I reluctantly bade her farewell, a little disappointed in myself for not breaking my health rules for a bit of adventure.

When I turned to wave good-bye, she summoned me back so that she could take a selfie of the two of us. I gave her my card and asked that she send me the image. A memoir of a once in a lifetime encounter. (Alas, I did not receive the image. My email address appears to give some mail servers problems, so maybe this was the why.)

FEB 6 The Josephson junction

An acquaintance for some years now, **Malcolm** spotted me as he walked past the coffee shop I was sitting in. Of course, he is not a stranger now, but he once was, and remains a little strange. Rather offbeat. He came in and sat down in the other comfy chair opposite me, seeking no signal that this was what I wanted. It was OK though. I will occasionally mention people who are no longer strangers as they still form part of the human web I like to connect with.

We chatted as normal, but I could tell he had something to share with me. He furtively brought out a printout of the abstract of a scientific paper he co-authored. I had a quick read, attempting to understand the subject matter and entirely missing the point he was trying to make to me. The research was carried out some decades ago, he told me, in conjunction with another Cardiff man by the name of Brian Josephson.

That man later became famous, sharing a Nobel prize for the development of an electronic device, which was subsequently named the *Josephson* junction. No wonder Malcolm was proud. His past was richer and more fruitful than the decades since where he has been medicated for a health condition that he constantly strives to dispute with the medical profession. He believes the diagnosis is false, but the 'system' and even his wife insist on him taking the drug. He can be a difficult man to talk with, as he hates small talk. But I can get close enough to his level to make it enjoyable.

13

Mia and her sister

I had arranged to meet my sister **Carol** for coffee and catch up. I got there early and became so involved in a chat with a couple sat nearby that I got quite exhausted before my sister arrived.

Fortunately I was able to maintain some semblance of sanity in the chat we duly had. My sister is pretty easy going so probably did not notice my rather drained state. After a short while, two little girls appeared at a nearby table and we both commented on how well these children related to each other, playing with such harmonious care and love.

Their parents soon arrived and this gave licence to the young one, three year old **Mia**, to come to my seat and ask me all about myself, her face so close to mine it was out of focus. Now this interest in complete strangers would embarrass most adults. But the most remarkable thing here about these children was the authenticity of their inquiry. **Mia** was clearly interested in my answers, not playing out an adult trained script.

When I gave her my contact card that sports a butterfly photograph I had taken, she was thrilled. She looked at me and gently asked "Can I keep it forever?".

My emotional nature finds such deeply felt words very sweet and moving. The pursuit of money in this world cannot make genuine moments like this happen, and can actually serve to numb and distance us from others and such tenderness.

Her six year old sister asked my sister the same kinds of questions.

A while later, entirely with the support and awareness of their parents, they took turns to sit in our laps. To lay down and cuddle. This was as deeply relaxing and endearing as it was strange and unexpected. A base feeling of contented connection was solicited. I asked the parents how they felt about this and they said they were equally friendly to all strangers they met. The elder child (whose name I forget, alas) was apparently shy until **Mia** was born. She effectively taught her elder sister to connect with others.

Some weeks later (date unknown), I met the mother and **Mia** again, but strangely failed to recognise either of them. I crouched down to **Mia** who also failed to recognise me, albeit briefly. When she remembered me, she took my hand and started to walk me around the coffee shop. I am, in such situations, as a child again.

14

My friend Ana in Spain

Whilst walking to the mini-supermarket near to me today I paused to chat with the homeless man sat against the front glass pane. It was easy to talk with **Bleddyn** (or maybe it was spelt Blethyn?) as his voice was as gentle as his face, infused with a lyrical Welsh accent. I often jump in conversation with strangers almost randomly to a matter of recent personal interest. So this poor, cold, homeless man was on the receiving end of chat about the practice of meditation that I have recently been reading about. In particular I talked about the concept of *equanimity*. This is the Buddhist concept of seeing pain and discomfort as a normal part of life and not to experience them as suffering. I wanted to share my curiosity about this matter not least because he had to personally endure daily suffering. So it was a lovely surprise to discover that this gentle man was entirely aware of these concepts, and indeed practiced them. Who would venture to believe that a homeless person would do so?

Later in the day I sent a link to the Youtube video of the brilliant rendering of "The Impossible Dream" song by Andy Williams to my friend **Ana** in Spain (an emotional, curious and friendly lady I met playing the game of Go on the internet). I talk of **Ana** as someone who is also now no longer a stranger to give my first example of the kind of coincidence that can arise when we talk with many people.

She loved the song!

She loved it so much, in fact, that she searched for other versions, such is that curious, explorative nature of hers. She shared one video where Peter O'Toole performed the song in "Don Quixote: the man from La Mancha". This is most odd as **Ana** actually lives in La Mancha. But stranger still was that when I was a young boy I was given a wonderfully illustrated *Don Quixote* book by my uncle.

How does such a wonderful double coincidence come about?

It is very easy to presume that it is simply by chance. But as my story will unfold, you will see that it happens more than it really should. I get excited about such coincidences, so detect them readily. But they still need to happen to be detected.

A few weeks later, **Ana** was involved in another coincidence ...

MAR 16   The author of a book

I discovered by chance a truly excellent book about human-computer interaction in a charity shop. As an ex-programmer with a nature attracted by elegant, ergonomic design, this book was very appealing to me, so I had to buy it. The particular version of the book was a few decades old but in immaculate condition, and a subject that is surprisingly timeless.

I mentioned the book to my friend **Ana**. Her seemingly insatiable curiosity made her decide, by chance, on a whim, to investigate just the first of the book's four authors – *Alan Dix* – on the internet. Quite why she should do this I have no idea. When she told me Alan was born in Cardiff the name started to ring a bell.

Without **Ana** nudging me, I would not have picked up on his name from the book cover, but I should have done so as it was now becoming familiar. I checked with my sister and yes, it transpires that he was in her class at school. She described him as a 'quirky genius' and it was no surprise that he should be involved in such a publication.

APR 12   Saxophone player

The Waterloo Tea Shop by Waterloo Gardens had its windows open on one side today with a vacated seat inside pointing out! So I sat and faced out into the hot sun. The couple sat at the table outside proved to be most friendly. He had been a musician in the Coldstream Guards for twenty-two years. She had a resplendent mane of ginger hair, scintillatingly enflamed by the sun. The image of her on the next page cannot of course show the vibrancy of light and colours in her hair. Another way in which taking with strangers is a matter of the moment more than for later replay.

Her hame was **Lara** and she was a Saxophone player and teacher. How very splendid is that! In the characteristic manner of someone with *ADHD*, I blurted out a word association – I asked if she knew *Supertramp*, the 1970's band with a distinctive saxophone sound?

Yes, she most certainly remembered Supertramp and told me a story about *John Holliwell*, their saxophone player. When the band finished touring, he decided to go to college to study classical saxophone. And in spite of his fame and experience, he was humble enough to start at the beginner level. Which is, as you might now have guessed, how **Lara** met him as they were on the same course! But how did I know to ask that question?

Lara

17

Mohamed

I found myself walking past a young man reclined on a park bench in Waterloo Gardens. He looked deep in thought so I asked him if he was a thinker. I am quite impulsive like that. Some can see it as intrusive, so I use an upbeat tone, and observe quite carefully how people respond.

Mohamed, aged nineteen, replied that he was indeed a thinker. At the moment I spoke with him, he had been contemplating the concept of *impermanence* – the finiteness of things and events in life. Such as his now drained bottle of drink. We chatted a while about philosophy, and he thanked me for taking time to engage in conversation, saying that few people do. I suspect if I had stayed longer, I would have learned greatly from this young man. At his age, I was affected by, and involved in more trivial matters.

Fedwa and two Ali's

This morning on my routine vigil to Coffee #1 Wellfield Road, I started chatting with a handsome young man with a beaming smile and the most immaculate hair. Fluffy and frizzy but immaculately organised. His name was **Kieran** and he explained how he exercises his Christianity through his football teaching. This I endorsed because this active, hands-on aspect of religions serves the public very well. He was excited by a forthcoming trip to Rwanda where he will practice this form of humanitarianism. Most crucially, he wants to show the way of Jesus through his behaviours rather than preach or evangelise. This was very refreshing to hear.

In Waterloo Gardens mid-afternoon I looked to sit on a bench, but first asked the lady sat there already if it was ok to sit next to her. **Fedwa** was easy to talk to with a charming smile, most happy for me to join her. Her son **Ali** came over and immediately asked my name and other questions. She explained that he was autistic. She had trained him to socialise and her efforts were clearly most effective. As is my way, I said I knew another boy called **Ali**, from Iraq. And, it transpired, this family was from Iraq as well. And it just so happens that **Fedwa** had just received her PhD in Physics and knew **Ali's** mother because she was also doing a PhD in Physics!

Her other two children returned to the bench from their wanderings. A boy, **Ahmad**, and a girl whose name I do not recall. I guessed that she was twelve. I was wrong, but very nearly correct – she will be twelve tomorrow. She had her mother's smile, and was a delight to meet and talk with. After twenty minutes, or maybe thirty minutes, I felt as if I was a part of this family.

Fedwa was a teacher before a career change, and carried her skills into her home where she taught her children to practice *sonics* to improve and refine their speech.

It was rather surreal to be so connected with these four people. I had, however, most irritatingly tensed up and acquired a small headache, so I decided to depart. I regretted not photographing this adorable family (absent her husband who had been invited to a meal elsewhere), but decided that it would have been inappropriate, and that some encounters are best experienced just once. To drag something special beyond its original expression can forever tarnish the memory of it.

Ali called goodbye from afar as I walked away.

I went to the Waterloo Tea shop to recharge and hopefully calm my tension down. I found a vacant seat outside – but in a trice an elderly man proclaimed he would sit at the same table. I was straining from my headache, so really wanted to escape into my book. And I was not keen on talking with someone who showed the signs of not tuning into others. But I chose to chat, and my concern proved very ill-founded. We talked for ages!

Eric was 87 and from Southend. Sharp, articulate and well informed. We discussed many things. Strangely, this did not exacerbate my headache, although I was rather tired at the end. His wife **Shiela** latterly joined us. One matter we discussed was the worry of his family that he is losing his memory. I made it clear that this was a minor malaise as he clearly had his wits about him. He wants to meet again to see if he can remember my name.

APR 19 — Two Liverpool lasses

I was sat in Coffee #1 in Wellfield Road in the front-most comfy chair – the best seat in the house when the windows are opened to allow air and sun to flood in – when a lady asks to sit in the comfy chair next to me. She proceeds to read a children's book that she is commissioned to review. So I also sit and read, but naturally more for fun than as a task.

Before she leaves, she offers a short but engaging chat. She is Indian, I believe, with an enchanting smile, along with a clearly high intellect, but one that is laced with pragmatism. She was so fascinating that I really want to chat with her again (at the time of writing, some five months later, I wait to encounter her again).

In situations like that, I find that I lose my sense of self and become infused with the person I am talking with. In a way, I become that person, *feeling* as well as hearing their stories. This energises me and I can get most terribly thrilled and animated, the child within me bursting with enthusiasm and excitement, making it easy to love the process of learning about someone else. The excitement of entering a life most unlike my own.

Yet I risk headaches as I did with **Fedwa**. They seem to start when excitement and enthusiasm is replaced by a feeling of entrapment – when a powerful sense of wanting to be elsewhere starts to grow, and simultaneously a feeling develops that it would be rude to leave too soon. Tension rises as I am pulled in opposite directions by desire and respect.

This reminds me of a chat with a very friendly Polish lady a few years ago on this very subject. She too really enjoyed the company of others but would feel this same urge to 'run away' from them when enough time had passed. She said that staying on felt very forced and painful. She was extremely relieved to know that this was not unique to her. Social anxiety in all its many forms is very much *not* confined to the few. My view is that it is a kind of collateral from our evolving genetics, where those who are socially tuned-in tend to sustain relationships longer and have more offspring in the process. But the social niceties can become wearisome – we can put aside our own needs and wants for the common good only for so long.

Later in the day I sat outside the Pear Tree restaurant with a pot of tea and a book, bathed by the hot sun. Close to me were two students playing chess. So we talked. **James** (I think that was his name) and I embarked on a discursive journey to everywhere our shared fancies took us. As if we had known each other for a long time. We even talked about psychedelic drugs and the changes they make to our view of the world. He declared that his personal experience of them created a paradigm shift that will likely stay with him his whole life. We also talked about Go, an Asian competitor to chess. I went home and returned with a book about the game as he was most curious to try.

I seem to be blessed with the luck of finding interesting people with bizarre connectivity involved. Later in the day, I stumbled upon two Scouse ladies who were sat on the floor absorbing the early evening rays of sun outside the Plasnewydd Community Centre (adjacent to the tennis club at the end of my road) before performing in a gig at the Gate Arts Centre across the road. Their group is called *She Drew The Gun*. I had to drag out the chat as I love meeting and talking with the people of Liverpool. I believe them to be the most natural connectors with strangers in all the land.

I mentioned to these ladies that I had been listening to the Liverpool group 'The Coral' this week for the first time in many years, having just downloaded it to my MP3 player. This associative jumping from one thing to another characterises the ADHD mind I have. Monty Python's Flying Circus even had a sketch on the theme that started talking about "Word Association Football".

I learnt that these ladies are managed by a member of 'The Coral'.

How crazy is that?

APR 21   Community football

Cardiff is the greenest city in the UK. Literally the most amount of green land per capita. The compact town centre lies one side of a road the other side of which is a park that dwarfs it for size. Nearer me is the large Roath Park recreation field where I have played games from frisbee to football since the early 1970's. A form of community football matches have been played there on Saturday's and Sunday's for decades, linking people from many countries around the world who have been to drawn to this city, mostly to learn or study.

I have participated in hundreds of these matches since 2000 when I moved back to Cardiff. They have been a fabulous way to get exercise and meet many, many people. Most notably, **Nao**, a sleight Japanese lady, **Jumbo**, a short, stocky Malaysian who played for his nation at the age of sixteen and **Francisco**, a Spaniard appropriately blessed with flair and skill.

Many players have come and gone, from all the continents, including a group of Mormons ((who played each week without any evangelising), and no less than three players from North Korea. What I have learnt from these encounters with strangers who became acquaintances and friends is an understanding of a common thread of humanity that runs below the cultural variations. Middle Eastern players can get heated, but likewise can be warmest in friendship, yet each individual is different. I learnt also that I felt a little uncomfortable standing very close to players like **Chivvy**, a powerfully built athlete with very dark black skin. The sheer difference felt a little alienating. But I really, really did not want to feel this. I want to treat everyone without arbitrary bias. So I let the feelings fade – and they did. It is now more likely that I will warmly shake hands with players from Sudan or Namibia than the few Welsh who attend. The latter tend to adopt the British aloofness.

This evening I sat on the bench facing up the field. It was 6:45 on a sultry hot sunny day. Implausibly hot. A good summer day in effect, yet it is clearly early Spring. No sooner had I sat down than two young men walked towards me.

They knew me from playing community football last year. Both were twenty-three years old, one from Morocco and the other from a country I cannot recall. Not content with a simple *hello* to someone two generations older, they engaged me in chat for maybe as long as forty-five minutes. They were fun and interesting, urging me to visit Morocco.

At the end, I got distracted by a boy about ten years old who was playing football on his own near to us. When the young men left, I risked my injured knee to do some simple passing with him. Even this simple exercise was indeed very risky, but so much fun!

This boy from Dubai was quintessentially polite and a delight to be with, along with being a good footballer. The connection with him felt like a brief intertwining of sensitive souls. He profusely thanked me for playing football with him. Afterwards, I watched him as he joined in a game with some other boys. It was not appropriate to photograph them but the low evening light was outlining their figures most delightfully. A golden fringe encased each player.

APR 22 Contact from Lara

I received this email from **Lara** :

I hope you don't mind that I should send you an email, and hope that you remember me, the red-haired lady at Waterloo Tea Room, about a week ago perhaps?

I had to tell you how much I enjoyed your book of photos, (my favourite being the pair of swans – you captured a fantastic shape) and that I am currently fully immersed in your other book, 'Think More' which I am finding a fascinating read.

I visited your web site, and discover that not only do you think, write, take beautiful photographs, but you make exquisite wooden pieces... and I am keen to know, are you still producing these boxes and chess sets? They are stunning! Please tell me more! Your woodwork is fantastic. I have yet to read my way around the whole web site, but I shall. I look forward to hearing from you and perhaps I shall see you at the Waterloo Tea Room again some time.

Best wishes, Lara

APR 23 — Sat on the park bench again

Once again, the sun lured me to the Roath Park recreation field bench, this time rather earlier at 4pm. The lady already sat there was basking in the sun. Her name was **Cerys** and she was wonderfully friendly. When she said that she was a business journalist, I challenged her on the matter of business ethics, to which she clarified that she was involved only in positive news reporting. We talked a while and also with her two girls, aged seven and twelve. She left and a lady by the name of **Sim** of Indian extraction replaced her. Again, a lady permanently smiling and terribly easy to talk with.

Brief moments.

Brief exposures to the lives of others.

Each new person like a new book to indulge in.

APR 26 — In the class of a billionaire

You may not like to talk to strangers. Or you may feel that you would not know what to say. What can you say to someone you know absolutely nothing about? The British way is keep things phatic (the converse of emphatic) and talk about the vagaries of the weather or some other neutral subject. We can actually sometimes get a bit animated in conversation if it is too hot on day two of a warm spell after complaining about dull weather for weeks. But often we lack a curious, connecting mind.

I feel that inquiring about the occupation of someone new you meet is a good starting point, although I like to make connections mostly from visual features. To point out how colourful their dress is. Or the precision of their haircut, much as I did yesterday to the son of a new neighbour. The boy's hair was immaculately, precisely organised, all hairs lined up like a Chinese military procession.

But it is vital that all engagements are honest and truly felt. When I remark on how someone looks, I mean it. It is essential to try to only say things that you mean – a kind of cognitive consonance.

I also really work hard at trying to adopt a related tenet of Buddhism. If you agree or offer to do something, then you really, really try to make sure that you fulfil that commitment. All too often these days, talk via mobile phones is cheap and commitments appear to be very laxly honoured. When you do ensure you will be true to your word, you will feel better about yourself, as others will also feel about you, knowing that you are someone to be trusted. I also try to adopt the Buddhist concept of acceptance – to treat others without judgement – a matter I will discuss further later.

This proved to be the third Friday in a row where I have experienced an unexpected and novel connection. It is starting to feel a bit surreal. And most likely it might appear implausible to you as you read on. But I stress that everything I write here is verbatim. Nothing is contrived.

The drive behind my desire to engage with others is paradoxically a consequence of being introverted. Let me try to explain. My introversion (and mild Aspergers) makes processes and matters of the mind very appealing. So I read books on a wide range of subjects. That itself is driven by a seemingly limitless curiosity, especially with the vagaries of human nature. But introversion, and the intrusion of headaches means that I spend vast amounts of time in my own company. Which in turn makes spontaneous, often brief meetings with strangers very attractive. Such encounters tend to have few social obligations, and can be disengaged pretty rapidly and painlessly. So they feel light and undemanding. However, they can turn sour when there is discord in the dialogue or when the encounter lasts too long. But in general, time alone makes meeting people with little social constraint very appealing. Almost paradoxically, meeting up with people that I know tends to be more socially prescribed and feelings of entrapment can ensue.

After finally having stressful home plumbing work completed, I went to Coffee #1 in Wellfield Road for a latte. I asked the man by the window if the other comfy chair was available. Fine, he said, but he was going shortly though.

An hour later, we were still talking.

We chatted about various matters, but especially about cars and roads as he used to work in transport. After a while, it dawned on me that he reminded me of an old school friend, *Ian Wilson*. I felt as comfortable in his company as I used to with Ian and realised quite quickly that he was also a bright, articulate middle aged man as Ian now is.

It was not until very late in our chat did I ask his age (he had earlier said he was retired). He told me that his name was **Tim Jones** and he was sixty-four, volunteering also that he went to Howardian High School here in Cardiff, the school my family attended. It transpired that he was in the same class as my brother and *Michael Moritz*, the now billionaire venture capitalist who invested in Google early in its life. He even went to Marlborough Junior school with him. **Tim** was able to tell me something about my brother I did not know. That his obsession with drumming expressed itself in lessons. Most likely *paradiddle* practice.

There was most certainly a sense of destiny about this chat – that I was somehow meant to meet up with **Tim**, and for him to feel very familiar in voice and nature. It was like a connection that was always there but only now manifested.

In the afternoon, I walked to Waterloo Gardens Tea shop. I sat with **Jose** from Portugal, a lecturer in sport at Cardiff Metropolitan University. I mentioned to him that a Portuguese family lived a few doors away in my street. Five minutes later, that family walked into the tea room!

So crazy!

APR 28 Talia and Lily

Talia is a delightfully natured and very beautiful young lady I chat with in the gym some mornings. She is no longer a stranger, but the source of some coincidences, as well as adviser on this book. When the sun catches her smiling, relaxed face, she sometimes looks like an A-list film star. Her beauty is wonderfully not just skin deep, as she has a very inquisitive, curious and analytical mind. The more I talk with her, the more evident this becomes. Yet quite where the curiosity comes from is unclear as she is also extremely calm and un-reactive by nature. She declared one day to me that there are times where she really should react to situations but just feels no urge to do so.

Each time she enters the gym, she projects tranquillity coupled with a warm, natural smile. I enthuse about this lady to many as I have not met anyone quite like her. I am not sure if her beauty in a way amplifies or maybe even detracts from the appeal of conversation with her. But I should not dwell on such matters and just enjoy her company. She is a dedicated Christian and knows that I am an atheist. But she neither evangelises nor judges. She can and does challenge some of my notions but is largely very, very open minded, respecting my views.

On this particular Sunday, I happened upon her in the park with her daughter Lily. A super vitalised creature, blessed also with a curious mind, and boundless energy and vitality. The photograph on the next page does not do justice to either of them – it was just a snapshot. But it captures Talia's honesty and nature in her face.

Talia & Lily

We chatted and met with her friends for about an hour, by which time I became most terribly tired.

The next day, we chatted in the gym. And again in the coffee shop afterwards where she found me. She had gone there to work on her degree dissertation. She declared that we were similar in nature. In some ways, surprisingly so. The next day we again chatted in the gym, and the following day in the coffee shop and then in the gym on the next day. Most strange to keep bumping into her.

Today I was in the coffee shop where she found me and told me a fascinating story with animation in her voice and sheer joy in her face. She is a delight to behold when she is like this, as she is a bewildering mixture of relaxed and excited. She told me that a few days earlier she had been walking her normal route when she felt God was guiding her to deviate from it. As she did so, a tree stump with bright green leaves growing from it appeared in front of her. She felt that she had reached her destination, but did not see any value in it.

Some while later, she found a book to research for her dissertation work and discovered on the cover was a tree stump with bright green leaves growing from it. Remarkably familiar, of course. This was indeed an amazing coincidence – and a delight to me that her joy at this matched mine.

Often when I tell stories to people, with energy and enthusiasm in my voice, as Talia employed when talking to me, their reaction is flat and one of almost disinterest. That saddens and deflates me. I mentioned this to her and she felt the same, puzzled that many people had a flat outlook on life, almost bereft of excitement.

Talia and I are like children with our sense of awe. The exuberance can be overwhelming for some, but we both see it as a precious part of our childhood to keep nurturing.

MAY 6 — My Brazilian friend Ramos

With a rare, super clear head, I decided to sit on one of the benches in Waterloo Gardens on a semi-sunny, cool-breeze day. But it was partly occupied. So I asked the lady sitting on it if I could join her. Her name was **Marie**, aged twenty-seven and relatively quiet. Not silent, but not seizing the initiative in our conversation, although she was friendly and accommodating nevertheless.

She was a photographer, just as I used to be, also photographing weddings as I did for four years. So we could talk about photography and the passion behind it. After thirty minutes or so, I was getting a headache, tensing up with the strain of trying to generate a two-way dialogue with a quiet person. But it was something I would repeat if the situation arose again as it was fascinating to see her come out of her quietude and open out. She said that this was often the case. She seemed to need to open out slowly to others, she said, like a flower opening its petals.

Ramos, my softly spoken Brazilian footballer friend appeared from nowhere and lightened my load. I must regale the story he told to me as I asked him then to tell it to Marie.

He used to work as a security guard in a bank in Brazil. One day, armed robbers came in, spraying bullets around like confetti. He needed his bullet proof jacket but was still hit in other parts of his body by no less than six bullets.

A true story.

He showed me the bullet scars one day after playing football.

MAY 7   Cheese snack

I merrily went out shopping for a new convector heater without thinking of checking store stocks first. The shop of course then had none to sell. So I walked to the bus stop for the return journey home with my tail between my legs, bemoaning a headache that had started during this trip. What gets frustrating is that I have no clear idea why that headache should kick off. But I had a babybel mini cheese in my pocket – a tried and tested way to assuage some of the effects of my headaches – so I was at least prepared for this eventuality.

A man laden with two large bags of dog food appeared at the bus stop. We chatted. He was a jolly fellow, but regretted carrying so much in one go. Within a few minutes of his arrival, he took a snack out of his pocket. A babybel cheese, no less. Identical to mine. And this was the first time I remember ever seeing someone take such a cheese out of their pocket.

MAY 8   A series of meetings

The day after watching a pulsatingly brilliant Liverpool inflict a surprise beat 4-0 win over Barcelona in the Champions League semi-final necessarily finds me tired but nevertheless still desirous of chats with people. I met **Declan** for the first time a little while back. A stranger quite happy to chat with a middle aged man. I saw him again in the coffee shop at 10am and asked to sit in the chair facing him. A gentle fellow, he recommended I read some books by Colin Wilson. He left after a while to do some writing and later in the day play with his band *Red telephone* at a Cardiff venue.

Here is a photograph of him taken from one of his recordings, appropriately sat in a chair much as he was in front of me today.

After he left I talked with a stranger named **Josh**, working on his laptop. He is writing a thesis for his Philosophy Ph.D. on the theme of order as it relates to religion. He is a 'nice' man from Texas with an accent sounding more Canadian than American.

After a brief chat with another Ph.D. student working in micro-biology, I want home and then caught the bus to town. On the journey a bearded fellow sat near me. I was in an energised (yet tired) state so asked him if he was following Ramadan (I guessed because he had a distinctive beard). Yes, he said, but it was hard here in Britain as the daylight hours were so long. He gave me a fist pump when he left the bus.

When it was my turn to leave the bus, my mind still wanted to chat with more people. Not sure why, but that happens occasionally, even when I am as tired as much as I was today. Other times I want to hide from people. And I mean, really hide.

I saw two 'Mormons' at a bus stop and took the opportunity to stop and talk. (In Britain, the 'norm' is to generally avoid engagement with them at all costs). They informed me that I was using a slang term – Mormon is merely the book they follow. One with a ludicrously long name on his badge was from Thailand. The other was a Napoli supporter from Italy. And not one word of preaching was proffered. We just chatted. They were a delight, each shaking my hand as I departed.

The energy and synergy of meeting such people, head state permitting, never seems to cease to excite me. It is most odd as I have a pretty low boredom threshold.

MAY 11   Applied meditation

I was pondering today on the place that *meditation* has in a healthy life. In particular, I was wondering how meditation relates to just doing nothing – the simple act of just resting. Additionally, I wondered how it relates to *mindfulness*, where we look at and respond more intently at things around us rather than letting them wash over us on autopilot.

In light of these similarly beneficial activities, it occurred to me that formal meditation is akin to gym work, but instead of strengthening our physical muscles, it strengthens our *attentional* muscle. The effect, when doing so, is to calm the endless chatter in the mind – to give respite from that endless bombardment of ruminations, worries and plans.

But surely, I decided today, meditation should also be a means to an end – what is it building our attentional muscle to do that might benefit us in our daily lives when we are *not* meditating? I thus decided that when we are out and about, it makes attending to the world – looking more closely at nature for example – more effortless. Our focus is less impulsive and more measured. We start to truly see what is around us rather than let it pass by superficially. We become more *alive* since we are more consciously aware.

Personally, I certainly find it hard to do traditional gym-like meditations such as focusing on the breath in the dark at home. Rather than find another isolated meditation to use to build my attentional muscle for a better daily life, I discover and invent my own meditations *within* daily life to do instead. I call these applied meditations. And there are a myriad of meditation/attention targets in the real world, from wonderful cloud formations to fluttering tree leaves to swirling bubbles in a cup of tea.

On a walk in the park, I can meditate on a flower, on the swaying of the branches of a tree, on the pattern of a weather-beaten brick in a wall, and so on. I train my attention at the same time as I apply that attention. My point here is to see meditation as a living, active part of daily life rather than some off-line, unrelated activity.

I also got to thinking about a matter I touched on last year in one of my thinking episodes. This is where I mull over a concept for a period of days to see it in many different ways and maybe understand it more deeply. To let it brew and yield more than was originally obvious or salient.

I concluded this time that many of our drives are *statistical* in nature – we get nagged often enough by our bodies to eat, for example, that we eventually succumb. The vital matter here is that such statistical forces have a *probabilistic* effect rather than an *absolute* mandate or effect.

So, with this statistical concept in mind, I decided that the endless chatter in our mind that meditation seeks to alleviate may also be a drive that lacks precision. It tries to get us to 'do life' even when we have time to chill as part of its statistical *coercion*. It tellingly often does overload us more than it needs to.

This puts meditation on a much more practical foundation, as it clearly helps fix a blunt methodology our minds have evolved. We really do not need to be endlessly concerned about 'doing' life, and can spend valuable time 'being' instead, and harbour no guilt that we are 'wasting our time'.

We slowly transform ourselves.

From *human doings* to *human beings* again.

The philosopher on the bus

I was nursing a little headache as I journeyed on the bus back from a small shopping trip to Waitrose in Pontprennau, trying not to get irritated by an intense conversation a lady was having on her phone a few seats behind me. She was quite loud and swore also. I was finding it hard to release my feeling of annoyance as it was exacerbating my headache.

I turned to share my angst with a young man listening to music who sat immediately behind me. He took the headphone our of one ear and we chatted. I told him that I was annoyed – questioning why she unload her woes so loudly in a public place – but also that I did not want to be annoyed at her. My tone was calm, at least, but the content of my words contained annoyance even though I wanted to try to retain the neutrality of Buddhist non-judgement.

He carefully and calmly explained to me that we naturally can only know this bus-side of her situation. That much may have happened at home before she got on the bus. Or that she might be struggling with ill-health. I knew these concepts but his perspective was valuable for immediately softening my stance. It made me ponder the scenario further, adding my own thoughts to his.

I suggested to this young man that the instinctive inclination to push such matters out of earshot may be driven by the wariness that her life may be worse than ours and that we therefore do not want to feel the full scale of her plight and possibly be burdened by the sharing of her problems. He agreed on this take so I instinctively asked if he was a philosopher.

Yes, he said!

He reads mostly Eastern philosophical works by *Confucius*, about *Taoism*, and Sun Tsu's *The art of war*, a book recommended to Go game players.

My stop arrived too fast and I sadly had to disembark the bus.

I did not know his name and very much wanted to talk further.

MAY 14 Bite worse than bark

The particularly fragile, anxious state that I was in this morning was precisely the wrong one for what happened near noon when I walked between two neighbours chatting in the street. For the first time ever, the little dog owned by one jumped up as I passed and sharply bit the back of my leg, drawing blood. The shock was hard to handle in my very fragile state.

The owner profusely apologised and gave me anti-septic treatment and a plaster. I went to the hospital accident and emergency department to seek treatment – on a day of truly magnificent blue sky and sunshine. So I was stuck indoors when I desperately wanted to be outside. The sun on my skin has a remarkable calming and relaxing effect – precisely what my anxiety yearned for.

They treated the cut and gave me antibiotic to take for seven days. What unbridled joy to see on the box that sun on skin must be avoided. Just as we are having a heatwave! Just when my anxiety was at a toxic level. Such moments in life I find particularly hard to handle.

But I had a nice chat with the lady waiting at the bus stop. No matter what the circumstance, talking with strangers – escaping the self – is often a way to distract oneself from pain or discomfort.

MAY 15 The untethered soul

This morning, I started chatting with a lady accompanied by her baby in Coffee #1 in Wellfield Road. I sat near the window but away from the sun, reluctantly.

The more we chatted, the more each of us became animated. We clearly shared the same passion for psychology and had matching curiosities of mind. She says she discusses such matters with her husband but finds few to talk with in public on such subjects. Her name was **Hannah** and she recommended that I read a book entitled *The Untethered Soul* (I ordered a copy when I got home) – a book about the Eastern concept that we are not our minds, bodies, thoughts or feelings, but simply awareness.

Hannah wanted to meet again, but because formalities even as simple as an arranged coffee with someone can trigger headaches, I declined and asked for another rendezvous to be spontaneous. She was fine with that and left me with a concept to ponder upon – curious, challenging minded people are likely to do that. She asked that I think about the nature of 'pain' and tell her my thoughts when next we chanced upon each other.

I found **Hannah** to be an amazing lady – really open, positive, animated, happy, supportive and passionate. That such a young person as this would actively choose to chat with a sixty-two year old is, on reflection, a little strange. So I probably particularly appreciate such connections in light of this. To be honoured by the young!

MAY 16 — That spontaneous rendezvous

I did not see **Hannah** in Coffee #1 in the morning – I was keen to chat again, but I was less energised than yesterday and felt a little anxious about being able to match yesterday's energy and enthusiasm levels.

Later in the day I decided to go to the Waterloo tea shop. After a while, sat in a window seat, I saw a lady with baby about to enter the shop. Normally I miss this as I am reading or my mind is miles away. And I am normally too lazy to open the door. This time I did open the door and the lady said as she entered "I'm not stalking you".

I actually had not recognised that it was **Hannah** again!

This was indeed most spontaneous, but I was anxious of mood and struggled to reach the fever pitch of yesterday's conversation. I felt myself tense up not wanting my lower mood to bring her mood down. She smiles a lot and I did not want that smile to fade as a reflection of my own unsmiling demeanour. I suspect extroverts do not think like this, but I may be wrong.

Anyway, after half and hour or so I bade her farewell and went to sit in the park. The sun proved to be quite weak, so I set off for home after only a few minutes. As I walked along the street I could see **Hannah** a short distance ahead, so sped up to join her.

I explained to her my strong feeling of needing to keep the conversation upbeat in fear of bringing her mood down, risking a reaction from her by talking in this deep manner. I need not have worried as she happily declared that she had not noticed my lower mood. This allowed me to relax deeply as we walked and talked, as if we had been friends for years. It was nice to expose my raw feelings, but maybe a little odd as I only met her yesterday. I discover that she lives in the next street.

MAY 20 — Catherine on her laptop

Another walk to Waterloo Gardens and the splendid tea shop, that has no less than *fifty* varieties of loose leaf tea. Green teas, black teas, oolong teas and so on. My favourite is Jasmine Pearl green tea from China. It is a most alluring place to sit and sup tea or coffee, as its busyness testifies. I sat near a lady working on her laptop. Her name was Cath, short for **Catherine**. She looks for jobs for disadvantaged people.

Even though she was working, she was remarkably welcoming of my conversational intrusions. She wore an endless smile that was quite clearly not contrived or appeasing. Evidently just a happy lady but also one with a really caring nature.

At one point she asked me if I had a son as the man her husband plays squash with was my *doppelgänger*. I was most curious. I will ask my friend Matt who is of that age and also plays squash. This is the same Matt I played tennis with yesterday ...

MAY 21 — Taiwanese psychology student

There is a recent new regular in Coffee #1 in Wellfield Road. A scantily clad and pretty young lady, Asian in appearance. Alas, I am still drawn to the 'eye candy' she brazenly presents, so I chatted with her a few days ago.

Today I talked with her again and found it an inconvenient distraction that she was wearing a low cut bra. And sad that even at the age of sixty-two, a confirmed introvert and bachelor, that my hormones still operate as if not. Fortunately, she has a similar spirit to myself, chirpy and upbeat in conversation. She was very happy to connect, and the more we talked, the more her appearance became displaced by her interesting personality.

From Taiwan, she is studying psychology, and was as excited by the subject as I continue to be. I gave her a copy of *Think More* to read. She was excessively pleased. But that over-exuberance was still nice even if extreme, in large part because it mirrors how I often react when exciting things happen.

Aoife

I took a different route on my way home from my shopping trip to Waitrose in Pontprennau. It was a very sunny day and I was practicing the centring of awareness, deeply influenced by *The Untethered Soul* book. It was taking me away from the 'story' my mind was making about the combined headache and toothache I was struggling with. Releasing the sense of suffering my mind's story wanted to impose was making me feel energised and drawn to a landscape that was illuminated by a bright, hot sun in a flawless blue sky. Quite a rarity in Cardiff.

At the bus stop, all four school children waiting were connected by sight or sound to their mobile phones. I asked the nearest me if it was mandatory that a mobile phone be used. She declared not and we started a delightful chat. She was a kindred spirit, astonishing, I feel, for a girl of probably sixteen years age. **Aoife** was her name. An Irish name pronounced *ee-far*. Like me, she declared herself to be an introvert keen to meet strangers. This surely cannot be a common theme at such a young age. She was calm and clearly intelligent. She was also an atheist, obliged to attend a Catholic school where she said she struggled to avoid the indoctrinating influence that religious infiltration had reached into the teaching she received.

I asked her where she got her independent thinking nature, realising as I did that it was probably born within her by its very own nature. She was not sure. We got onto the bus that duly arrived and I made a point of not sitting with her. I did not want the chat to end, but such a connection and dialogue with delightful people are probably best kept short and sweet, or allowed to take a natural and finite path. Being attached to them is not a good idea, I reasoned. She was pretty, and therefore pleasant to talk with, but that was kind of beside the point. It was her nature that was most pretty.

Later on, I passed another local supermarket and paused briefly to have another chat with **Bleddyn**, the homeless man with a gentle demeanour who was sat on the floor outside again. No longer a stranger even if not yet a friend. But he too is part of the human web that integrates all who wish to partake.

Pentwyn leisure centre

The gym I have attended with a rare level of consistency for some nine months now, where I seek to retain a reasonable level of fitness and muscular protection for chronic knee problems is closing until June for refurbishment. The leisure centres in Cardiff are run by *Better*, an independent not-for-profit business. Access to one gym gives access to all. So I caught the bus to the Pentwyn Leisure Centre, a few miles away. My first visit there I believe. The lady at reception spoke with a familiar West London accent, so I inevitably asked her where she was from. Many of her family were born in the same Hillingdon Hospital as myself. I asked for directions to the gym, and was told to go upstairs and walk past the indoor bowlers to access it. There was just one other person in the gym, but I did not enjoy the session as the brand new quadricep and hamstring machines they have here had worse ergonomics than the ones I am used to in my regular gym.

I caught the 57 bus home. At the traffic lights, opposite the Penylan gym, a man tried to flag the bus down. The driver refused. But this clearly determined man operated the outside open-door button. Which was then closed by the driver after he stated that he could not pick up now in the traffic-light queue. The man outside got angry and took a photo of the driver which he claimed he would put on social media.

I said to the young man next to me that he was too angry. This young man asked me which – the driver or the man? We chatted about it, and much like a few days before, and on the exact same section of the bus journey, my view was challenged by another young person. I happily conceded that I was being biassed in favour of the driver's perspective. We chatted further, in part about anger itself, and how he is calm and un-reactive in nature while his younger brothers are on short fuses. He was due to join the Navy and hopefully travel the world. I wished him well. When I stood up to leave he made a point of shaking my hand and thanking me.

This was a true delight.

Mid afternoon, I sat on a bench in the park. A man a few years older than myself stopped to chat. He did, however, talk rather at length about his bodily ailments. But I was fairly patient. I should be more patient, but patience remains a 'work in progress' for myself. Before leaving, he mentioned that he had played indoor bowls this morning. I barely had to ask to learn that it was in Pentwyn leisure centre. I suspect I had walked past him this very morning.

MAY 25 — Scrabble challenge for my sister

Saturday often means coffee with my sister **Carol** in Coffee #1 in Wellfield Road (as should be clear by now, I rarely tire of visiting this cafe. I have no financial interest in it if you wondered that). Of course, she is the least eligible person to be in a book about talking with strangers. But I will mention people I already know from time to time for matters of coincidence and human web connections. Today, she had the story of a twenty-five year delayed honeymoon to recount. She and her husband **Dougie** travelled Club Class to St Kitts and Nevis islands for a rare luxury holiday.

One day in a lounge area, a lady was heard asking if anyone wanted to play Scrabble. As an avid player, my sister of course was happy to take up the challenge. But she was soundly beaten – something that rarely happens to her. She met the lady again a few days later and chatted more with her, only to discover that her name was *Annie Freud*, a poet, and daughter of painter *Lucian Freud*, and great-grand-daughter of *Sigmund Freud* the famous psychologist. How cool is that?

MAY 29 — Shopping at Marks and Spencer

There are times, of course, where my meetings with others are less exciting. Even uncomfortable. But this is to be expected and to be taken in my stride. Today, I needed to buy new underpants. My life is full of such excitement. So it was that I ended up in Marks and Spencer's, an iconic British institution. They had a set of four briefs for £18. Or a set of five plain cotton briefs for just £8. I really could not tell the difference. My waist size is 34", but I like my underwear a little loose. So I bought the 36"-38" briefs and then sat in the coffee shop with a medium latte. On my own, with nothing to read. And, it seemed, no one to talk to.

I meditated and also started observing the water droplets skitter down the window pane – the vast window pane – that overlooks the main shopping thoroughfare outside. And I got to wondering if these droplets slid down the window or rolled down. It is a consequence of a curious mind that I might ask such a seemingly trivial question of myself. Meditation increases the chance of questions about life beyond the confines of my mind and body.

Since they were tear shaped, I presumed they rolled down the pane. (I later found research papers on this very subject, would you believe, and this is the likely answer to my question. But droplets will roll or slide dependent on the angle and friction of the surface).

Eventually, a lady asked to sit at my table. A bold, loudly spoken lady. She told me that she did not marry until she was thirty, but was now married for fifty-eight years. So this eighty-eight year old was the oldest I have spoken with so far. But she was very much not eighty-eight in mental faculty. And when I solicited a laugh from her, the yip of sound she produced – much like a dog bark – was so loud and fierce that it hurt my head. But I wanted to engage non-judgementally, so I let my 'pain' ride. Taking her on face value, as it were, also meant trying to work out which of her eyes was the lazy one, as they did not both look in the same direction. Oh how our minds can react to discomforting experiences!

But I warmed to her. She said that her husband wanted to read so had gone to another coffee shop down the road. And she was entirely happy with this. Clearly a lady in command of both her faculties and emotions. And the more I spoke the more the piercing laugh diminished in effect.

Alopecia

The briefs were still too tight!

So I walked back to 'Marks' as we tend to call the shop. I bought the 39"-41" size (and they were a comfortable fit, even if technically 6" too large). The man who served me had less hair than me. And much greater height. Attired all in black, he was a most commanding presence. But I noticed that he was more than bald as there was no sign of any hair on his head whatsoever.

So I mentioned this to him, and he of course informed me that he had *alopecia* – hair simply did not grow on his body. Anywhere.

This of course meant that he also had no eyebrows and I said that this must be a problem in the rain. Sure, he said, but also in the gym, where he was forever wiping away salty sweat to stop it rolling (or maybe sliding?) into his eyes. I said it must be tricky managing this impediment but he said that he was very philosophical about it, realising that many others had much worse problems.

I left with a strong recommendation that he reads *The Untethered Soul*. When reading books that grab my mind, I tend to promote them to all and sundry.

JUN 1 — Matt and three ladies

Saturday morning and (yet) another trip to a coffee shop. When you are retired and live alone, such venues are a godsend. Few who work realise how very tricky it can be to meet people when not working. I wanted to read in a seat that was soaked in rare sunshine. But **Matt** sat nearby, with **Naomi**, his girlfriend, and he had been hoping for a chat with me, it seems. So I put my book aside and sat and talked, catching up with his progress. He is a great guy, and always worthy of attention.

He used to work in this coffee shop until about five weeks ago, before which time I used to regale him with snippets from books I read in the cafe. After doing so for many months, it was clear to me that **Matt** was the most mentally healthy person I feel I have ever met. Easy going yet not in denial about realities that can hurt. A very authentic fellow with a comforting smile. Always that smile, even if suffering with a hangover.

One day, shortly before his days in the coffee shop were over, he was slightly pale of face and not smiling. Something serious must have been afoot. I asked and he said he had a sharp pain in his stomach.

I learnt the next day that after a while he went to Accident and Emergency to be assessed, and thereby learnt that he had a ruptured appendix! They said he must not eat before the operation to remove it. This was in the afternoon and he had only eaten breakfast many hours ago. And the operation, he was now told, would be in the morning. Pain was therefore now coupled with raw hunger. The poor lad!

Next time I saw him, he told me about the operation and that he would be in Casualty. Again, I asked? What do you mean Matt? What happened?

It turned out that he had subsequently been interviewed for a new job on the production of the television programme "Casualty". Today, he said that at the end of June he was promoted to a new role where he would work on site on live sets. Twelve to fourteen hour days while filming, followed by light office days. He said that the group he will work with get on so well, have such great chemistry, that the directors are really happy.

In the afternoon, I set off on a walk around Roath Park Lake, stopping on the way to sit in the sun and read. At least, that was the intention. I sat on a bench adjacent the rose garden, next to two ladies, and a third soon joined us. We chatted for about half an hour. The eldest lady, **Rita**, sat this side of the other bench declared that she was not Scottish when I asked her. She was from Dundee, she proclaimed. She was like the comedy actress *Maggie Smith* in her Scottish role. A quite hilarious and engaging talker.

We chatted about Brexit, observed the children playing and walking past, about the value of peer support in schools, and other matters. **Val**, the lady on my right on my bench was from Middlesbrough, and was keeping up a regime of walking around the lake each day in order to lose weight. She used to be a youth worker.

In these chats, **Janine**, on the other side of, and daughter of **Rita**, was mostly quiet, but occasionally sniggered. It would appear that **Rita**'s tales were not always robustly accurate, let us say. At one time, **Rita** was saying that she had to go to a memory institute, so I swiftly asked if she remembered the appointment. Of course, she pronounced, only for a smiling **Janine** to correct her. She had indeed forgotten.

I would love to have videoed this chat, but capturing it would somehow have diminished it. Many young people forget to enjoy the moment, becoming too obsessed with capturing it on their phone. I do not carry my phone with me.

Vertigo

Well that was a first! And of course, I very much hope the last.

Lying in bed last night I felt dizzy and unstable. It was a strange feeling. I opened my eyes and the room moved back and forwards as if I had been spinning around and had just stopped moving. Except that I was just lying in bed. Left or right side, the shifting sensation was scary and seemed to want to deny me any hope of sleep.

I sat upright and it all went away. Except that my brain was now freaking out about what had happened, and extrapolating to a night completely devoid of sleep. And that meant a panic attack, including cold sweats. Having learnt to relax in such situations (as much as that is possible when you feel terrified), I was able to observe this sequence of horrendous feelings and let it pass without getting fazed. I was deeply impressed with the sheer power and scope of the ways my subconscious can make me feel dreadful. And that access to the subconscious to switch this off was utterly denied my conscious mind. Proof again that we are not one mind but many – Marvin Minsky described it as a *society of minds* in the title of a book of his.

After a couple of hours the problem went away and I fell asleep, but got up at 7am feeling pretty wretched. I had breakfast and walked to the surgery to join the queue. The man in front of me was very relaxing to talk to. Kitted out in gym clothing ready to get his exercise-induced endorphin fix after seeing the doctor.

When he reached the reception desk, he declared his date of birth as the 18th of February 1956. I told him that this was precisely one year before mine. How odd. Maybe we could chat so well because of that. When the receptionist saw me she addressed me as Mr Moffatt. She had overheard our chat and had looked up my details in advance.

The doctor said I had suffered a bout of medical vertigo where the ear canals get false signals. It may come back though.

Doh!

JUN 5 Brummie man

I embarked on a long walk to Roath Park and around its lake. On the way, I chatted with a man in a motorised wheelchair. A very friendly fellow, close to my age, who sounded uncannily like the Birmingham comedian *Jasper Carrot*. So I mentioned this to him. He said that Carrot used to catch the same buses as him, and wrote sketches about them. He did not personally meet the man, however. Now that might have taken things too far. If you can, watch Jasper Carrot joking about moles. You must be able to find a video of that.

JUN 6 Matt on set

First time this year to travel by foot and bus to Penarth, a small town adjacent to the city of Cardiff bay. I stopped on the way for a chat and read in Cardiff Castle grounds with eternal gratitude to Mr Bute, once the richest man in the world, for bequeathing the Castle and grounds to the citizens of Cardiff. So we can apply for a pass giving us free access every day we choose.

I had a brief chat with a lady from Adelaide, which was followed by one with a bubbly student of medieval history who had Spanish and French accents flavouring her fragmented English. Sometimes, with people like this, it is not easy to tell if they are happy to chat or are just pleasing the audience and would rather move on soon please. But these two people seemed entirely comfortable talking with a complete stranger.

I did eventually move on, catching that bus into Penarth, walking down to the sea front for some sunbathing before embarking on a stroll of a mile or so on the grass embankment running above the pebble beach shoreline. As I set off, I noticed on the beach a familiar figure from the coffee shop I frequent. A ginger haired lady who is bilingual, speaking a mix of English and Welsh with her two and four year old children, sat while they played on the beach. The *only* people on the beach! I went down the steps to say hello, and sat a while. The four year old gave me her normal big smiles, but did not poke her tongue out this time.

My knee complains about these long walks, yet seems to really benefit from them. So I pay little heed to the pain. The clouds forming as I walked were a dazzling mix of shapes and formations. It is only occasionally that I capture them, but I simply felt compelled to take photographs this time. However, I had to frame around a man on the fringe of one of my shots. We happened to stop and talk later, meeting further along the trail. We discussed religion … and then clouds! Can you believe that he has had a long term passion for 'cloudscapes' as he called them. Today I could understand why as you can see in the photographs I took on the next page.

Before I met him, however, rather menacing grey clouds intruded and cast a dark shadow across the land. Ahead of me, as I walked, I saw what was clearly a film crew, huddled in vans and under canopies by the cliff edge. I took a photo and walked closer. The man charged with managing public intrusion walked towards me.

Maybe you guessed already that this was a filming of part of a "Casualty" episode and my friend **Matt** was the person approaching me. I guarantee that this and all other stories are true. Why would I want to contrive this and put it into a book? But I really had no idea he would be here today. It was good to chat with him. Always so mellow.

The young lady on the set was connected, under her clothing, to a safety harness. In the filming that now took place, she lost her footing and fell part of the way down the cliff edge. An actor at the top shouted out in alarm. End of take. There must have been at least forty people in attendance, but only a few operating the camera jib that lent right out over the cliff edge to film the fall.

Catrin

JUN 10

With grey clouds building overhead today, I nevertheless decided to walk to Waterloo Gardens. Normally, I reserve such trips for sunny times. I sat at a table outside with my Jasmine Green tea (oh what such a delicate creature of habit am I) and read until spots of rain forced me inside. A chair was available next to a lady with striking wavy blond hair. I wanted the chance of a window seat in case the sun came out, so I looked fondly at that chair. Probably too conspicuously because she welcomed me to sit next to her.

I was tired and not really well prepared for what followed – an intense conversation with one of the most energised, enthusiastic women I have ever met. Probably the most *alive* woman I have had the opportunity to encounter. After a while I told her that I felt inert in comparison!

She too sat in the window because she adored the sun. She too was a sociable introvert, but often mistaken as 'flighty'. Her immediate impression hid a lot, but some of that, especially her deep thinking, started to show the more that we talked and the more that she opened out to me.

I was chatting with **Catrin** (a very Welsh name), from Aberdare. She is principally a choir instructor, but not a 'normal' such instructor. She teaches singing in schools and even in hospitals. It is worth noting that some terminally ill cancer patients have their lives extended as a result of the vitalising effect of group singing. She is also a song writer and corporate entertainer. And she has sung internationally.

But her openness and humbleness belied all this. We talked of various things, before turning to meditation, a subject that was clearly of mutual interest. After one year of daily practice, she claimed that she had reached a peak, one day, where she had complete silence in her mind for about a minute. This may sound quite trivial an achievement (you just try and see how long you last), but afterwards, the effect upon her was so deep and profound that she felt as if she had been on holiday.

I said that there was a book she must read. I started writing *The Untethered Soul* book title down on the little notebook I carry with me in front of her. Before I had finished writing, however, she shrieked. This book was next on her list to read. She had only just bought it!

This happened precisely as I describe it.

She declared a sense of destiny.

Also, it has to be said, that it remains odd that a tired, sixty-two year old balding man can captivate such an energised person without coming close to matching her energy levels. I have to repeat that sentiment as almost everyone averts their gaze from me when I walk down the street. I do not mind nor blame them but I am not someone people tend to seek out in general.

Catrin was also a surprisingly great listener. Quite the rounded person. Quite the most amazing lady. Quite the most perfect example of the danger of judging others on their appearance and behaviours.

JUN 12 — Cardiff Bay crafts gallery

I attempted to catch the bus from Cardiff to its airport in order to hand out copies of my thinking book to passengers with the premise that they might actually read it in the long hours a flight offers them.

I checked the bus stop location on the internet before setting off, but actually completely forgot where it was by the time I arrived in town and ended up walking all the way to Cardiff Bay in search of its starting bus stop there. But I simply could not find it. You might think that this ineptitude would be a rare matter, but it is sadly not. Me failure of memory frequently lets me down, yet, paradoxically, it pushes me to think more to compensate.

Whilst in the bay, I took advantage of my locale and popped into the splendid and capacious Art and Crafts gallery. As always, it had a genuinely wonderful array of brilliant paintings, sculptures, jewellery etc. One lady was seeing how ponchos looked on her. She was dressed in bright colours, so I mentioned how nice she looked. She said that she was an artist visiting the UK with her husband who was at the Cardiff Hilton hotel for an International Society for a *Hyaluronan Sciences* conference. This city was chosen as it has pioneered in this new science. (Hyaluronic acid is an important component of articular cartilage, as I later learnt when I looked it up on the Internet).

I presumed that she was American rather than Canadian, a matter that still is hard to be fully sure with my British-trained ear. I did however have a guess by her accent that she was from California, and I was amazed to be told I was correct. She too is an artist, and an introvert, but entirely friendly and chatty. She said she started wearing bright colours to make herself more cheerful. Either it was working, or, as I would guess, she was a cheerful type anyway. Again you see an example of how often we misjudge how others see us.

JUN 13 · A smattering of chats

It seems that *The Untethered Soul* is a popular book in South Wales right now. I sat with **Louise** today, a counsellor and Reiki master, and bubbly, smiling empath by nature, who is currently reading the book. From the way she refers to it, I suspect it has had less of a profound impact on her than it has had on me. But there I go again – judging someone. So easy to slip into that habit!

We chatted about mental health and education, and that the two are necessarily coupled. Our government is hellbent on exercising the 'small state' ideology by cutting education, school, prison, police and other budgets regardless of their current status. Mental health patients with no bed to use end up taking an NHS bed instead, so the problem with one system can end up overloading another.

What was obvious to Louise, myself and millions of others, that holistic, joined-up policy making seems to be utterly ignored by the politicians in Westminster. Sad times. But a delightful lady.

In the afternoon, I took the 58 bus to Pontprennau in North Cardiff to shop at Waitrose in part because I had run out of turmeric root for the curries I make every day. As a Caucasian White man, I am pretty unusual in preparing and cooking a curry from raw ingredients every single day for thirty-two months now. I never seem to tire of eating them.

I got my free cup of tea and sat at the cafe bar, on a high stool. A man soon joined me. His name was **John Hancock**, I was to learn, and he proved to be splendidly friendly and informed company, a fellow sixty-two year old, born 2 months before me. His opening gambit was that we were privileged in this country to have had sixty years without war and plenty of amazing progress. But the 'party' as he called it, was nearly over, as we have been trashing the environment. It was something I had to agree with. It is clearly something that we must all be deeply concerned about.

John was not a pessimist at all but a realist. We talked about politics and education and also health since he was a doctor whose role was to provide career therapy, or some such like (I am terribly poor at remembering terms, I am afraid). He helped people with in-work health problems. So he was delighted that I gave him a copy of my *Improve Your Life* book. I said to him what I say to you now. I promote my books as a way to give to or help others. He said that many who suffer with mental health problems might find my book useful. He got me to sign it, which was a bit awkward.

JUN 17 A promise to heal my knee

The lady sat in the corner of the coffee shop today was clear-faced and energised. She went beyond a simple hello to chat further. From North Wales, she had that lilting Welsh accent that is laced with a proto-Scouse tinge. It was most disarming and relaxing to listen to. When I talked of my knee pain she quoted from the Bible :

Isaiah 54:17 "No weapon formed against you shall prosper"

Sian promised me that if I cite this I will be free from pain. I have, as yet, to try, but am somehow not terribly confident that it will work. But I accept such advice with as much neutrality and gratitude as I can muster, resisting the urge to declare my atheist position this time. **Sian** also recommended that I listen to YouTube videos on the Holy Spirit by Derek Prince. I will do so – it is good to challenge our innate tendencies to fall into the confirmation bias trap and avoid what challenges our mindset.

Later, back in Waterloo Gardens, I talked to a Mum with the youngest of her three sons. A relaxed, smiling lady, easy to chat with. She said, without seeking any kind of pity, that her first son was born with *Coeliac's* disease, and her second son had a 'heart plumbed in the wrong way around'. He had to undergo major, life saving surgery. Maybe these ordeals made this lady stronger, I am not sure. Maybe she was able to deal with what life offers anyway. But terribly hard for her all the same, yet she was taking life in her stride as far as I could see.

I received a reply from Catrin!

Hello Neil,

It was so lovely to chat to you at Waterloo Tea last Monday.

I met with the gardener and we've made a plan to tame the garden, it's a big job as the garden is meadow grass rather than a lawn, so it's gone quite wild ha ha. He's booked in tomorrow to start the job. Phew!

How wonderful that you sat next to a counsellor and reiki master, and that she is mid way through "The Untethered Soul". I'm also midway through, though I decided to listen to Michael.A.Singer's lectures to see where his mind was at before I started.

He's such a great talker and very funny. You're right, the book is perfect for me, and it especially feels right for this time in my life and where I'm at on my spiritual journey.

I must say I absolutely loved your book. I read it right through in one go like I said I would. It's so incredibly thought provoking. As I told you I love to meet new people and get to know their stories, and this gave me the opportunity to do that. Such wonderful stories. The interweaving story with Sarah, John Vector and Dr Rowan Williams led beautifully to the Summit, and what a perfect way to end with 'The World Questions'. It's filled with life lessons and left me asking more questions, and exploring the people in my own life.

I loved the ideas within the stories painted throughout the book, the wonderful moments, acts of kindness, changing of one's path, the relationships. The story of Enid and Henry was so beautiful. I truly believe in self healing, and when I first lived in Cardiff I was in a car accident and had back problems, so started seeing a therapist, where I started CBT, but she also introduced me to Louise Hay and Abraham Hicks, the books 'The Artist's Way', 'Ordering from the Cosmic Kitchen' and

'Mind over Mood' which was the beginning of my spiritual journey.

I'd like to say Thank you for giving me your book. I do believe people come into your life when you need them, like angels almost. 'The Untethered Soul' may have sat unread if I hadn't met you, and I would never have received 'Balancing Act'.

I've attached some acoustic versions of songs I've written, I haven't released these online, but thought you may enjoy them.

JUN 21 A state of bliss

Today I had a most sublime walk in Bute park, adjacent to Cardiff Castle. A strange thing has been taking place with my meditations, and that manifested in an entirely novel way today.

The basic idea behind meditating is to give us a break from the endless rumination, worries and planning chatter in our head. That internal, eternal, nagging voice driving us to be busy. It takes conscious effort, at first, to focus on something, such as the breath, without the chatter egocentrically urging us to pay attention to it instead. We must observe and not engage with the chatter, returning instead to the intended focus of our attention.

For some reason, I have always struggled to focus on my breath. It always seems rather awkward, the act of observation disrupting the rhythm. Instead, I tend to focus on a detail of wherever I am in daily life. An early such focus was the cluster of bubbles swirling in my cup of tea in a coffee shop. One bubble will break, and there is a pause before the other bubbles regroup. It is an amusing, cute little meditation target. The more relaxing the target of meditation, the more effective it generally is at training attention.

Another meditation I discovered is to stare at the wrinkles in my hands. Looking close – really looking rather than seeing – I realised I never have looked properly at my hands before. Quite a landscape, with craggy skin and plump, bulging veins. Not reason for alarm or matter of vanity, but simply a calm observation of reality – the details of which that often wash over us. (Eat a single square of chocolate very slowly, letting it melt on your tongue and you will go beyond habit eating and discover a richer experience).

These meditations expanded to embrace cloudscapes, trees, flowers, decaying bricks. Whatever. There was no set pattern to them. Some days I did very little meditating. Others were infused with many mini such meditations. And now, in the last week or so, after about three months of meditating daily, something has changed. Instead of the endless onslaught of 'doing life' chatter, my subconscious now gets me to stop and 'smell the roses', as it were. It actually takes over the consciously determined pauses to meditate by starting them itself. This felt pretty profound.

I have not read about this takeover process anywhere, but it can hardly be a unique thing, even if most novel and vital to me. Today, however, the flow of automatic meditations lasted hours! I had a rare complete freedom from headaches and was in a very calm state. The sun was shining and all of nature in the park was bright and colourful. So it felt appropriate to find myself having to walk ever slower to yield to these urges to meditate. At one point, a squirrel stood looking at me for a few minutes. I was quite content to remain stationary, looking also above at the sun flecked leaves. They were transformed into the most magnificent spectacle by this calm, deep attentive, aware state. A myriad of colours and patterns. My vision, at age sixty-two, strangely immaculate.

I eventually stopped walking and got a cup of tea from a large cafe in the centre of the park. I asked the lady serving me how she was. She was surprised to be asked – I suspect few customers do indeed ask her. We talked about how she is learning Romanian from her co-workers. The nearest such Romanian lady seemed to be afflicted with a permanent smile as she joined the conversation. Most delightful. Such simple pleasures that many people rarely seem to value, understand or instigate.

I sat on a bench with my cup of tea, partially spilt along the path as I did not take a lid, and talked with a man from Yorkshire with a strong accent. He was a water engineer for the NHS. I asked if he worked at the macro or micro level. Both, he declared, his main focus being on lowering bacteria levels in water pipes. I talked a little about how nature used turbulence where engineers tended to avoid it. A flawed attempt to try to relate. But he was easy going and very accommodating. Kind of makes me want to visit Yorkshire again.

Later, on my way out of the park, I saw a lady sat alone on a bench. With a film camera, rather than a digital one. This is pretty unusual so I asked her about it. An American voice replied, but I learnt that this friendly lady was from the Ukraine. We talked a little about the laziness that digital cameras can inculcate, but I was getting hungry, otherwise I might have asked to sit on the bench with her. My timing on opening chats sometimes leaves something to be desired, but they are probably a consequence of allowing spontaneity.

JUN 22 Lloyd on the bus

The sky was blue and the sun most hot. Quite unlike Wales. But most welcome. I popped into the community garden adjacent to the bowling green at the tennis club at the end of my road. A lady I felt I recognised was picking strawberries. I was mistaken, but there was something still familiar about her. Or maybe, as I since reflected on the matter, it was because she was beguiling to me. Sleight of body, gentle of face, and the charm of her expressions and lure of her eyes drew me into conversation with her.

Even at my age, I can be attracted to ladies, even if I never ever now seek companionship. Her name was **Vida** and she was also, it transpired, a photographer, and even taught the film photography. I sustained the chat as long as was safely plausible. I was mesmerised by her femininity – the gentleness of her presence – and decided I would seek her company again some time. I went home to get some photographs to show her, but she had departed before my return.

Later, on the bus home from a Welsh festival in the town centre, I sat at the top front of a double-decker bus. I never cease to delight in the vista this offers. But also never cease to get frustrated by young people wasting the view by obsessively looking at their mobile phones. The young man on my right was speaking, with some calm authority, into his phone. This felt different. When he finished, I said to him that he sounded mature. He replied that he did not know how he sounded as he could not hear his voice as others do. How profound a reaction from someone so young?

He was sixteen, and a keen rugby player in a land that cherishes this sport. One that is, to my sensibilities, insanely dangerous for the body. As is clear, I have a certain anti-rugby bias, and the poor young man gave testimony to that danger as he had already torn ligaments in his feet playing the game, that took months to heal, and had been concussed no less than four times. Dangerous but a clearly compellingly addictive sport. I said I was writing a book about people I meet, and he asked if he would be in it. So yes, you are, **Lloyd Thomas**.

He was about to embark on a course of 'A' levels in Maths, Physics and Psychology, not so different from mine, in Maths, Physics and Art. I gave him a copy of my "Think more" book, but was quite unsure whether he was interested or not. But the next stop was mine, so my decision had to be made fast.

JUN 24 Betty

After my 9am gym session, as is my want, my luxury, my habit, I walked the two minutes from the community centre housing the gym to Coffee #1 in Wellfield Road to partake of a pot of tea. Two pots actually as they give free refills.

I asked an elderly lady if I could sit in the chair next to her – the always favoured comfy chair adjacent to the window. That I hog too much. I yearned again to sit there just in case the endless clouds decided to part and allow the sun to shine through. I bought a book about the sun yesterday – "The Healing Sun"– as it is a great relaxer and vitaliser in my life and I wanted to learn more, maybe discovering why it seems so vital to my sanity and health.

This poor lady had a walking stick by her side, and I discovered that she was awaiting a knee operation. Clearly, **Betty** was carrying a fair bit of weight, so I presumed that her need for surgery was greater than mine. Proof in front of me that I should not get too upset with a long wait for my own knee operation.

Before she left, she asked if I would help her get across the road. Of course, such assistance is good to offer – it makes me feel useful and reminds me about the plight of others worse off than myself. Helping her out of her chair was an immense effort. **Simon**, one of the staff, rushed to assist, then held up the traffic as we walked at a slow pace across the road to where her car was situated. She was appropriately grateful, and thrilled when I spoke a little Welsh – clearly her first language.

In such situations, **Simon** comes into his own – he is wonderful helping others, including children and dogs. He could readily work in a nursery or care home, and always seems ill-placed in a coffee shop, with its focus on indulgence and repetition.

JUN 25 Synchronicity!

I have been slipping lately into a relatively mindless repetition of daily activities. Not entirely unconstructive and not without interest or pleasure, but rather narrow in scope. I also concluded that I was not spending enough time being available in coffee shops and the like to meet others. So my plan today was to spend more time just sitting rather than reading in these shops. And yes, clearly this is a kind of luxurious lifestyle, especially as my headaches have been relatively low level recently.

54

After a while sat in the window seat in Coffee #1, a friend saw me and walked towards me. A vision. A beautiful, smiling vision. I told her so.

She talked about the bible verses she reads and copies to her notebook as a way of really feeling their import. I tensed up a little as she proved to be quite a strident lady who breaks the 'safe-distance' rule. And she challenged me, in a way, to become more accepting of the virtues of Christianity. I did try to listen though with as open a mind as I could.

The warm, open radiance of her smile reminded me of the doll character in the "Toy Story 4" film I saw yesterday afternoon. At one point in the film, when held by a child, the expression on this doll's face was one of supreme bliss and openness. The beauty and brilliance of the image of that face would be impossible to surpass. I am not sure many who watch the film would fully see that perfection. My mind screamed loudly in joy at the beauty, my eyes welled up and tears ran down my face. Muted sniffling in a cinema.

Later, a couple sat down near me. He was wearing all black, including an eye patch. I had to ask of him about this colour scheme choice. I suggested, when we spoke, that he might try a thin colour accent to accompany the black. He felt that green might work well. An artist by name and nature, **Paul Painting** was sitting with his partner **Nancy Jim**, both *environmentalists*. Warm, caring people as you might see on a GreenPeace boat on the television.

Without knowing about my stranger stories, he recommended that I read "The 7 Secrets of Synchronicity" book on the presumption that it might change my life as it had done to his. Quite why I had not yet read about the subject of *synchronicity* before I am not sure as it describes what has been happening to me in some of my encounters. Yet this man had no idea of how pertinent his book suggestion was as this was the first time we had met. (I later looked at this and related books and ordered instead a copy of "Living in Flow" by the wonderfully named Sky Nelson-Isaacs).

His partner, **Nancy**, came over a while later to talk, and share her web site with me. British born, with parents from Hong Kong, she sat facing me with an authentically warm, smiling face that was a comfort to observe. So it did not matter that she also broke the normal, socially safe talking distance. Sat close to her face, I felt a calm reassuring presence. I gave her a copy of "*Balancing Act*" to read, and she was delightfully thrilled, agreeing also to read it in one go as I suggested. She said that she was highly influenced by Eastern ideas, and wanted to bring that to the 'Sovereignty' here in the UK. To the mainstream mindset I guess she meant.

When I encounter people like **Nancy** and **Paul**, I feel quite honoured, genuinely so, that they give of heart and word so readily to a complete stranger. Compare and contrast with some people I pass in the street who look with silent disdain at me when I say hello. Alas, access to her web site timed out and I did not receive any emails from them.

JUN 27 Lucy in Pontypridd

A rare day blessed with constant clear blue skies, and therefore hot sun. Sadly, this was tempered by twenty m.p.h. winds. But I had felt compelled to travel – to make the most of the day – so went ahead and caught the 58 bus to town and then the T4 bus to Pontypridd, just North of Cardiff. It hurtles down the dual carriageway, sweeping past Castell Coch on the right, a fairy tale castle hoisted half way up a hill.

Pontypridd is a delightful town blessed with a wonderful park that even sports a Lido. The people have an accent far removed from the sharp Cardiff brogue, yet only twenty minutes away by bus.

After sun and lunch, I meandered around the park, taking yet more flower photographs. After two years, the ability of my Panasonic T1000 bridge camera to capture the brilliance of colours faithfully still lures me into taking more pictures. Of flowers. So often of flowers.

After buying the Michael Palin book "Erebus" in W.H.Smith, I sought a tea shop. And the one I found was as if trapped in time, the inside like a classic painting, or film set, 1930's in appearance. Yellow light was streaming down from the windows at an angle, illuminating perfectly a man sat alone with his coffee.

I asked the lady sat outside if I could sit next to her in the only outdoor seat left vacant. Her name was **Lucy** and she proved to be delightful company. Pretty in a distinctive, unusual way. But ever so much more beautiful when I was able, on occasion, to tell a tale that captivated her attention. The photograph she let me take failed to fully capture her essence – even when converted into a watercolour image.

She is a professional photographer, born of Hungarian immigrants to South Wales, now sponsored to create a photograph-based documentary of these immigrants in their 100's arriving in Cardiff, Newport and Pontypridd. (A National Assembly for Wales "Many Voices, One Nation" event in September 2019 to mark the first twenty years of devolution in Wales).

Lucy was also learning to meditate, but like me struggled to do so via the breath. So I keenly explained my plethora of daytime micro-meditations. She was relieved that there were other ways to meditate, saying how very much she loved to explore new ideas, wanting to try many things, so was very pleased to remove what was a barrier to meditation for her.

It was most odd, as we chatted, that I could never tell how she would react to my ideas and stories. Some times, her response was quite flat, but other times she hung onto every word, her eyes creasing up and dimples appearing in her cheeks as her face came alive.

By the end, the heat and the chat near-exhausted me. But it was a delight in spite of these problems. I gave her a copy of "Improve your life" to read. Maybe I will see at the Senedd in Cardiff where her documentary will be exhibited.

JUN 28 Nantgarw

I decided to visit Nantgarw, the village I passed through when returning from Pontypridd yesterday. The image of shafts of sunlight piercing through the trees yesterday was luring me back. A small town, it is blessed with some fine buildings, nestling on a hill below Castell Coch that I inevitably walked up to visit.

It was on the bus home that I chatted with a mother about her love of art, and then, after she disembarked, I found my attention turned to a couple to my left. They were making it clear that they were uncomfortable with the stream of students walking along the main road, who in their words, were 'all Chinese'. I pointed out that this was a matter they could not be sure about. This couple then demonstrated a classic fear of 'other cultures'. They were concerned about how many there were in this line of students. They were fearful that 'there were of so many of them', it seemed, and told me that these were extremely wealthy students as they knew someone who somehow knew about their bank accounts.

I listened but found it hard to accept. They seemed to be very negative and close-minded towards people they really did not know. And this was sad. I chose not to say to them that I had had Chinese and Japanese girlfriends in the past, not terribly keen to see them squirm and maybe pass judgement.

Talia again

It was a pleasant surprise to see **Talia** in the gym on this grey-clouded, cool, windy day. She was smiling radiantly, as always. I normally complete my gym schedule by 9:40. Today, it was 10:30 when I left, and I clearly must have spent three quarters of an hour talking with her.

This girl, as I mentioned before, is a radiant picture of health, happiness and beauty. But this is also a problem, with men near her age finding it near impossible to 'just be friends'. She and I talk about this as she likes to copy my habit of talking to strangers. Doing so, she necessarily lays herself open to misinterpretation. A lot.

Yet she does do this, and has tales to tell her friends that result from meeting new people in various places. She implored me to write in this book that her friends have also started greeting strangers – that I appear to have had a catalytic, cascading effect. This is so nice!

The "Living in Flow" book arrived today and I started by only reading the cover and forward. My head was sore and I wanted to start reading in earnest when my mind was clear and receptive. But it boded well – a Masters degree Physicist offering a scientific basis for flow and synchronicity. Yet he talks in a grounded manner, wishing to steer clear of some of the more extreme territory offered by the "Law of attraction" genre. Let's see.

Robert

When retired, the minutiae of matters like which coffee shop to go to, and if the sun is going to shine enough to sit outside loom far, far larger than common sense would say they should. Part of you knows that others have to work hard and rarely get the luxury that is your daily fare, but still, trivialities become unreasonably large, lying behind which is a kind of vacuum of meaning that was previously occupied by work. It is proof, if proof is really needed, that the mind is constantly comparing this day with yesterday and this week with last week rather than seeing how good things are in an absolute sense.

So today, if you let me say, it was the 1st time in a while to sit in the Wellfield Road Coffee #1 garden for a soya latte. And the first time to sit near a smiling, super friendly Romanian called **Robert Oros**. A published photographer, studying for his masters degree at the University of South Wales. His speciality is raw portraits of people, absent their makeup and often absent their clothes.

He had three books with him, and asked of me that I read a poem from one of them. It was interesting, but I felt unsure I could say anything appropriately profound about it. But **Robert** was easy going, and ever smiling, so it did not matter. He had a disarming nature, yet, he declared, he rarely chats with strangers. I found this hard to countenance.

He told me of a fellow Romanian he found himself talking with back in 2009. He asked where this man lived and was told in a small village called *Lliva* on the France/Spain border near Andora. Which was precisely where Robert had been the previous day. That very village. Spooky!

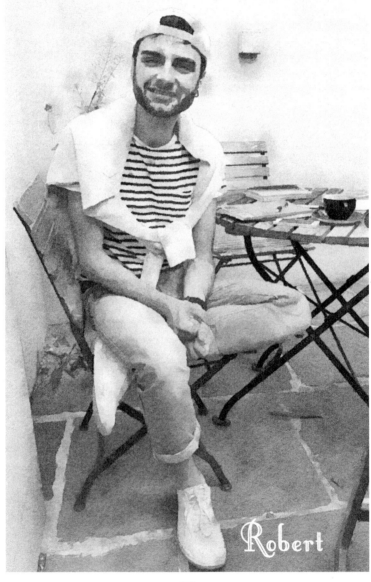

Robert

Dean at Cardiff Castle

Some people I open out to have stories ready to relate. This can be nice or tiring. It is very much a lottery. So it was at the Cardiff Castle entrance today, where **Dean**, one of the officials, regaled me with one such story in the first of these categories. Years ago, he said that a French government dignitary swiped his embroidered hat. Quite why, it was unclear, but **Dean** allowed him to keep it. Five years later, **Dean** was bemused to see the dignitary again, along with his hat, which was presumably being returned to assuage a guilty conscience. But **Dean** kindly let him keep it.

I sat to read deeper into "Living in Flow". I still find it remarkable that I was only now learning about synchronicities. An example from the book should serve to illustrate how apt this book is for me, so far, on this strange journey meeting strangers :

> *A colleague of the author (Sky Neslon-Isaacs) named Elsie was applying for a PhD post, but was placed on a waiting list for her first choice. Sky suggested that she could improve her chance of success by contacting the University. But she was sceptical of his belief in enabling synchronicities to happen. Eventually, she did ring and found that the acting head of the Physics department had gone to school with her mother's thesis advisor. This familiarity of capability was enough to move her up the waiting list and get accepted in.*

The point that Sky made here was that ringing was not a *causal* factor in this appointment. Her *family history* was. And ringing allowed that history to come to the fore. By embracing possibilities – by ringing just to see – a possibility line was opened. Sky relates these thoughts to a branch of the *possible worlds model* that is key to quantum mechanics, the theme of his Masters degree.

The book remains interesting in large part because of that Physics basis, and also because it links *being in the flow* (the Csiksgentmihalyi concept) with synchronicities. For sure, when I personally become engrossed in a rich, engaging conversation, I lose my sense of self and become the flow and also become the connection with the other person. It does feel like this enables strange 'coincidences' to be teased out. Staying flexible and free from expectations is also key. How thoroughly I agree with yet another person trying to commandeer quantum mechanics to explain the macroscopic world is another matter, however.

Chatting with Irish and Iraqi people

I found myself sitting on a Roath Park bench next to an elderly lady at 3pm. An Irish lady, up for the *craic*, the Irish term for a good old chat. Clearly a smart lady, most articulate and interesting. And very proud also, her son collaborating with a 1st class Tokyo University Mathematics student on his PhD.

During the chat, this very long chat, I discovered that I had tensed up without really knowing I was doing so. But it was certainly the consequence of a tendency to be overly effortful in conversation – overly diligent in order to avoid the type of social clumsiness that afflicted my early years.

The ensuing mild headache lasted the rest of the day. An irritation that was a 'punishment' for trying to be too nice, or simply a result of my efforts to concentrate when my mind actually wants to drift away in day dreams, maybe. It was uncomfortable rather than painful, just adding a grey, pulsing layer between me and the world.

I did not let it stop me enjoying my walk as I resumed my way, stopping to greet and talk briefly with an overtly smiley family sat on a bench. They reminded me of the two families from Iraq in my street – extraordinarily accepting and accommodating of me, with near permanent smiles. This family were also from Iraq, the father the first to arrive as a refugee, his wife and children following. They have yet to master English to the level that he has. The joy they showed to me made me feel that they were not often spoken to by the 'natives' of Cardiff.

Tamsin

To Waterloo Tea shop again! Yay! I sat outside after ordering my default Jasmin green tea, and basked in the sun. Behind me, through the open window was a lady reading a book. So it was a little rude of me to start to chat, although she seemed to be happy to be interrupted as she proceeded to enthuse about the Christianity book she was reading entitled "Garden City: Work, rest, and the art of being human" by John Comer. She also recommended "God has a name" by the same author. Later in the day I ordered the first of these books.

She told me her name but I sadly forget. I need to concentrate better when I ask, my mind too readily intent on moving onto the next part of conversation. I soon explained that I was an atheist but attempting to be a humanitarian and to follow a spiritual path. The chat was energised and she was so wonderfully enthusiastic that I could not help but be charmed. She and her husband had fostered a boy and loved him so much that they went through the process of adopting him. And now she finds herself pregnant with her own offspring.

After she left, a mother, daughter and friend of that daughter arrived. Instantly I could sense a very rare sign of connection, for they nearly sat at my table asking politely first if that was OK. But the other table was soon vacated, after hugs with the occupants who happened to be the former teachers of the daughter, **Tamsin**.

I asked if she and her friend were sixteen, on the premise that they looked young. But they were both surprisingly both twenty-one. **Tamsin** has worked as a camera loader in TV and film productions for three years, often working twelve to fifteen hour days, an insane norm in this business. To her eyes and mine, it smacks of sheer laziness for that industry to have reached this state.

Now you have to remember my age and that **Tamsin** was a pretty young lady, but one clearly overtly enthusiastic about engaging with strangers. This habit evolved for her at the tail end of the journey she had followed. She explained that her friends had gone to University, making new friends, while she was too tired and had too little time at the end of mercilessly long days to do so herself. She found herself lonely and depressed at the same time as she was being bombarded by 'better experiences' on social media that she could not partake in.

So she embarked on a journey of self development. And the result, I have to say, was one profoundly energised, curious and engaging young woman. She could comfortably out-talk me, but in a captivating manner. I think that she is the fastest talker I have ever listened to, albeit on matters that she clearly realised I was interested in. This lady was sharing rather than bombarding.

And once again I found myself in a photo with a twenty-one year old, along with her mother. They insisted that I be captured thus. I then took my own photograph as you can see on the next page. **Tamsin** is on the left.

I gave her a copy of "Improve your life" as I felt it might flesh out some of the things she has learnt. She was delighted. It is very easy to give out books when such is the response.

When I told my story about **Lara** and her saxophone lessons, **Tamsin** pulled me short to say that her mother had recently bought her a saxophone and she is learning to play.

Curiouser and curiouser.

JUL 9 Thinking about synchronicity

I had a gentle chat sat on a bench in town with a retired lady named **Clare** from Kent, and later a little lunch-time chat with another lady whilst eating a particularly dire and over-priced lasagne and vegetable lunch in a department store restaurant. As one of ten children of a farmer, this second lady had fond memories of drinking freshly squeezed cow's milk. I wondered if her natural sociability was kind of inevitable with such a large family. Probably not, I hedge to guess, as the quiet type might simply escape the mayhem and remain a quiet soul.

The book on flow and synchronicity describes a combination of techniques to use to both bring you into the flow of life and also increase the chance of synchronicities. The methods and attitudes described are essentially very much what I discovered by chance. At least partly so. My strong belief is that they evolved in myself from an adoption of the mindfulness and acceptance that I have practiced for a number of years now.

The notion of *acceptance* I mention here, an Eastern concept, is to recognise that what has just happened in life has indeed happened. We may

66

not like it, but we should accept that this is how it is.

We might indeed have crashed our car.

That is a reality we may face one day.

First, we accept that reality – we mindfully pause to observe that reality. Second, we determine what we should do, without being encumbered by an instinctive emotional reaction to what happened. So we let anger fade, and start to talk calmly with the driver of the car we crashed with. He or she may be angry, but we are better placed to talk with him by being calm.

Coupled with acceptance is *non-judgement* of others. You accept others regardless of how different they are from you. This counters the deeply seated tendency of the brain to pigeon-hole all that we meet, and treat those who are different with caution or hostility. Instead, we seek to accept difference without judgement. This lightens up our approaches to others – we can emit and feel an accepting and embracing attitude. We open out to others by not judging them.

This lightness of engagement does not mean a superficial one. By removing appraisal of someone we meet, we can listen and observe more deeply, and as a consequence we can more meaningfully connect with them. Part of the beauty of this is that when this accepting, connecting, non-judgemental attitude is sensed, strangers tend to open out to us in a virtuous manner that can reflect back that openness.

This same lightness of judgement can allow us to avoid attachment to how things should be. So if we find that someone we speak with steers the conversation to places we have not been before and have never been interested in, we still follow.

We do not so much abandon our own interests and agendas, but rather allow the dialogue with others to supply the steering, in effect. When the subject of their chat triggers something of personal interest, or aligns with our own current agenda, then synchronicities can become start to happen.

At least, this seems to be the case.

John and daughter

A few weeks ago whilst walking along Wellfield Road I passed a man who was clearly allowing his daughter to stop at every point of interest along the way. I spoke with him to commiserate. He explained that it can take them two hours to travel the short distance to his relatives, so slow was she. And also, quite obviously, how soft and conceding was he.

A few days later, the two of them appeared at my tennis club. Not as members, but simply to use the rest area between courts to play. At one point, they sat on the floor facing each other, rolling a tennis ball back and forth. Except that she was clearly not playing fair as she often let the ball go past. She simply did not seem to care about the game or connect with her father. So he had to stand up and retrieve the ball each time. We chatted, and he said that she was rather like her mother – his ex-partner – 'doing her own thing'. As soon as the girl was born, her mother had no interest in parenting her. So he took over and has had custody ever since, I believe.

Today, we passed in the street, and I asked his name – **John** – and told him mine. As is the nature of my ADHD, grasshopper mind, I immediately told him that **John** was the name of my father. To which he said that **Neil** is the name of his father. I love such symmetries.

He enthused about the books that he was reading and how he wanted to lend some of them to me. I love to be receptive to new reading matter, so look forward to seeing him again at the tennis club. I can give him one of my books also.

A rugby connection

I arrived slightly early for my regular meet up for coffee with my sister **Carol**. After finding a seat, I spotted and chatted with **Hannah**, so nice to see her again after too long. It has been far too long since we chatted.

I told her that I was meeting up with my sister and her son **Andy**, and that she should chat with him as he is an interesting young man. **Hannah** had good news to share – a new job as physiotherapist for the *Scarlets* Rugby team. As ever, her face lit up in excitement. And she chatted with **Andy** because, you see, **Andy** just happens to create a series of hugely popular YouTube Welsh rugby video compilations. So they were swiftly embroiled in a chat about players they both know well, but from different perspectives of course.

Jane and Elin

Back to Waterloo tea shop where I had a gentle chat with another mother and daughter, **Jane** and **Elin**, the latter an anagram of my name. **Jane** works for the Department of Work and Pensions, which has come under intense focus in British politics in the past few years. She oversees health assessments of disabled people, and therefore I really wanted to try to find out if this most nasty of Conservative governments really is operating an agenda that tries to deem even the most desperately disabled members of the public as eligible for work. But she seemed too nice to ever follow such a line of inquiry. What she did say served to ease my concerns somewhat. Maybe it is less of a problem here in Wales.

I gave a copy of "Think More" to **Elin** who declared that the trap of mobile phone dominance I describe on the back cover described her to a tee.

Farqid and Ben

Part of the dreary, but sometimes excitement-punctuated routines in my life is to catch the bus to Pontprennau and shop at Waitrose. I get my free hot drink and sit at the coffee bar before the shopping chore is undertaken. Today, I sat down with a cup of tea and "The value of everything", a book on economics I got from the library, whose thesis was to propose a fairer wealth distribution by defining *value* better than it is now. For example, GDP is boosted by money spent mopping up an oil spill, but no account is made of the vast amount of time people spend caring for family members. Value as a concept has been rather corrupted. Currently, the richest sixty-two people in the world have a total wealth equalling the poorest 3,500,000,000 people on the planet. An obscene inequality.

But I barely read a page as **Farqid**, the smiling gentleman who now sat on my left was keen to chat (his name must be pronounced with care...). A full time worker at an Arabic church in Cardiff, he was keen to preach Christianity to me. Especially when I revealed that I did not have a belief in God. This spurred him into full-blown evangelising. I did not mind too much, and stayed relaxed enough to intersperse some humour and other tempering measures to avoid a build-up of head tension.

But it was ostensibly a one-way communication. A monologue.

It seemed to matter to him not one jot that I might disagree with him. Nor that he might be misguided. But people working in churches do not just evangelise, so not knowing what else he did, I avoided judgement. He was a friendly man, from Iraq, with a Welsh wife. And an endearing smile. Yet another delightful smile!

Early in the evening there was a knock at the door. The lively fellow in front of me when I opened it asked if I was Steve. His name was **Ben Mott** and he had a very distinctive accent, a kind of disarming, relaxed dopiness of patter like David Beckham, so after telling him that I was not Steve, I had to ask him where he was from. Uxbridge, he said. West London. So terribly familiar as I lived as a boy in Cowley just a few miles away from Uxbridge. And of course, even though fourteen years younger than me, he went to Bishopshalt, the same Grammar school that I briefly attended (more on this school later).

I told him to call next door where the Steve he was seeking was staying. **Ben** was trying to resolve a leak problem with the builders across the back garden from me where a gutter was not in place during a day of solid, professional intensity Welsh rain, creating a leak in his girlfriend's house.

JUL 21 Clumsy in conversation

Sunday morning on my way to Coffee #1 in Wellfield Road, I found myself accompanied by a lady walking by my side carrying a box and sporting a delightful smile that necessarily caught my attention. From Turkey, with a degree in Maths, she was walking (just a few feet more now) to the new 'Blossom' vegetarian restaurant she was opening soon. I held the rather stiff door open to let her in, a convenient excuse to experience some more of her enchanting smile. Clearly not one that many mathematicians would sport (is it a form of racism to say this?) She also creates 3D designs. I said I would tell my vegetarian sister's family about the restaurant. So I anticipate eating there some time soon.

Behind me in the Coffee #1 shop queue was a lady wearing shorts just as I was. It was a mostly dull day so I commented on her optimism. Then I realised that she was athletic looking, told her so (I do like to say what I see), then immediately asked if she was a footballer. She seemed to have the right physique for that. I was correct – eight years a professional footballer, now playing for Reading in the Woman's Premier league. And then I did something I still regret.

I remain baffled why I did it – maybe she was just receptive and open minded – I can only think that impulse got the better of me. My ill-advised question was to ask her if lady footballers chesting the ball felt pain. It was a genuine question that had puzzled me for years, but still one not appropriate to ask someone you just met. Fortunately she did not slap me, but proudly declared that they did not feel pain.

How can I undo this question if I see her again?

JUL 22 Brain aneurism

A particularly enchanting, energised and ever-smiling member of staff who often served me at the Cardiff City Centre Coffee #1 shop seemed now to be in a bad place. Each time I saw this Romanian lady out in the street (I have not been to her branch this year yet) her face would be a little severe, absent that relaxed smile.

So when I saw her at the bus stop on my return home today, I was a little wary about saying hello. But I did. And I was glad I did. At least in a way, for her story was scary. She is the lady on the Coffee #1 web site home page :

Some months ago, she was diagnosed with a brain aneurism (I do not recall her saying what lead to that diagnosis). Before they eventually operated, blood had seeped into her eye sockets to make her blind for three months. She said that she had learnt some humbleness from this traumatic period – especially to really cherish life.

A vein was operated on to stem the flow to the brain that was causing the problem, the aneurism was fixed and her vision was restored. She was clearly calmer, her previous ebullient nature now more tempered.

Her eyes were pretty as before, but a shadow of the worry and scare she had endured for so many months was still present in her face. Until she smiled, that is, and I was offered again a glimpse of where she was and where she will return to.

When we parted, she made a point of declaring how tenuous life was. And therefore how precious it is now. It is sad that most humans only truly appreciate life when adversity threatens to take it away from us.

JUL 24 The big fat surprise

Now I have reached the point where I am actively seeking someone to talk to that I might be able to write about here. Not really what I wanted as it can narrow things down, corrupting the process, damaging spontaneity. But I headed for Waterloo tea shop on the off-chance anyway.

In the queue I overheard an old lady say to her younger companion that she had to be careful that her energy level did not drop. I risked an adverse reaction by interrupting to ask if it might be a blood sugar problem, and if so to look at trying high fat food as an experiment to stabilise it. They listened keenly, but this was contrary to their experience, courtesy of decades of National dietary misinformation, alas, but they were keen to explore this idea. Supremely receptive to a new idea when clearly relatively old. I hope I am like that at her age.

I later suggested that she should also check for possible thyroid problems, and to read "The Big Fat Surprise" book on the matter of dietary fat and the regime of misinformation. A book that took nine years to research and write that I cannot recommend highly enough.

To Pontypool

JUL 26

A roasting hot day. The high due to be reached today of 30C is a rarity in Wales, so I set off on a fairly long set of bus rides to Abergavenny. But I only got as far as Pontypool, alighting to explore the delightful park and to seek food to fill a craving stomach. The town, by contrast, was unfortunately a mere shell of its former self. Lots of low-cost and empty shops. A sad sight as the frontage to the town was blessed with a number of magnificent buildings such as this domestic property:

On the return journey, I spoke to a lady waiting for a bus. In contrast to my skinny frame, she was quite buxom. It is good to talk to people whose very form takes them on different paths in life. When I asked if she had the day off I discovered that the path her life had taken her made mine seem rather sublimely fortunate. She had had a recent period of rough sleeping (but was today beautifully dressed and well made up) and dealings with a council that was largely useless at helping her with the *paranoid schizophrenia* that she suffers with. She was in the middle of a two hour 'release' from a psychiatric ward.

It was hard to fully grasp this as she was gentle, warm and caring. Either I was misjudging her, or she really was very authentic, not hiding her inner nature. The first thing she said to me was to ask about my photography – she saw my camera and connected with me via it. In spite of her plight, her focus was on others. I was facing the low sun, necessarily lighting my face. It solicited these words, showing her forthright nature, and making my day :

"Your eyes are very blue. Bluer than blue."

We sat apart on the bus to Cwmbran where I planned to stop midway on my journey home. As we travelled, I was determined to say to her at the point of disembarking how very warm and friendly she was. Alas, she was ahead of me in the queue to leave, I got distracted, and by the time I dismounted the bus, she was vanished from sight. I searched around and she was nowhere in sight. I was a little upset as I felt that words of encouragement might have been a kind of antidote to possible paranoia plaguing her mind, or, more likely, the low self-esteem that mental ailments can foster.

JUL 27 With Indian and then Pakistan people

Often, my days are kept quite simple to maintain flexibility and allow for spontaneity. I have a distinct and painful aversion to overload. Today was a kind of overload but fortunately I remained calm throughout, which was nice as much as it was rare, especially after troubled sleep. A week ago, I had been stung in my abdomen by a bee or wasp. A four inch diameter raw, red, stingy, burning reaction lasted for a few days. Last night, it returned bigger than before, the pain/discomfort waking me through the night.

But I felt surprisingly fresh. In Coffee #1 in Wellfield Road, I sat with an elderly lady whose face was immaculately illuminated by the sun as we chatted, making her look remarkably beautiful in spite of her years. I told her so, not for effect but because she kind of really needed to know she was nice to look at and hence talk with.

Then to the tennis courts to give some rallying practice to my friend **Sally**. The pace is relatively gentle, allowing me to sculpt and tune my shots in a way mostly denied by the speed of the ball when playing against men.

After a while, an Indian man and toddler appeared in the seating area behind the court. When **Sally** and I rested at one point, they walked slowly, unannounced, onto the court so that the toddler could play with our tennis balls. A part of me felt this a little rude, but I let that fade as I realised that it was a rather petty judgement that served no meaningful purpose. We can hear these 'fussy' voices in our heads without choosing to pay heed to them. Do you realise that parts of your brain say things that really do not serve you well, and therefore need not be heeded? They often operate with trivial agendas that we can and should pretty much ignore.

Instead, I spoke with the man and then laid down on the ground to get to the toddler's level. We rolled balls back and forth gently until a smile emerged. When doing this, I lose my sense of self and become the person I am trying to connect to, even if only one year old!

After the tennis and lunch, I watched my long-term Pakistan friends **Mo** and **Haris** play tennis for a while. They had not played for maybe six months, but were rusty for merely minutes. It takes me weeks to regain my timing and rhythm after a break, but it is ludicrously fast for them.

There was plenty of time, even on this busy day, to walk to Roath House Church for a Summer fair, a very British thing. Families were playing games in the grassy garden as if we had been transported back a few decades. It was a delight to be absorbed in, and again, absent the intrusion and dominance of mobile phones.

I spoke with two Pakistan ladies and they asked if I would play a form of badminton with the husband of one of them. We used big soft paddles and a light ball. He was a seasoned badminton player but I was at least able to rally a little. When I sat down, his three year old daughter came over to me, it seemed, to simply offer a smile. She was a delight (maybe I should visit Pakistan also), and soon urged me to play 'tag'. To chase her and for her to then chase me. She delighted in this of course but I tired rapidly.

By now, I felt part of their family.

The wide openness of their acceptance of me was remarkable mostly in how natural it felt.

JUL 29 The Homeless World Cup

Day three of the *Homeless World Cup* football tournament, held over eight days here in Cardiff. There was, sadly, very little promotion of an event, a spectacle, that truly mesmerised me. The wonderful colours of all the fifty teams from across the world, where each player is or has been homeless or in drug rehabilitation, mingling amongst the public, practicing on sectioned squares for all to see. Three pitches, each with grandstands. And all free.

This was my second visit and I stayed for over four hours, bumping into friends, and chatting with some strangers. I said hello to **Aziz** who was seated behind me in one stand. He was a very friendly calligraphy artist, seeking to publish a book of his work. It was a thrill to see how terribly animated he became when describing how computer paint programs can enrich his work with textures and shadows to his heart's content. He had a stammer, however, and I felt both that I did not make him feel relaxed enough, but also that I wanted to help him with this blight. I chose, though, not say anything about a matter outside of my understanding.

I marvelled at the South Africa men's team, drawn passionately into watching their singing and dancing. Here they are :

76

Clearly, they were united as one when they sang and danced, not needing to look at each other to synchronise their movements. An automatic choreography. They played football with the same cohesion, and won all their first group stage one matches.

After watching Pakistan beaten by Portugal, **Ahmed Nawaz,** the president of the Pakistan Physical Education Development & Peace Foundation asked if I would mind sending him some photos. Of course! Except none turned out well, so I will take more in the following days.

Because this was a non-ticketed event, there was a relaxed feeling in the crowd, and one of tangible connectivity. If you get a chance to attend one of these World Cups, go!

Struggling to chat with strangers

On the bus on the way back today from shopping was an example of where I can struggle chatting with people. A 'loudly' spoken but very chirpy man boarded, and I became ensnared in his chat. I had a headache that I was trying to contain by meditating on the trees passing by, but he paid no heed to my blatant returns to window gazing. I tend to feel bombarded and trapped when someone does not tune into how I receive, or fail to receive what they say.

A fellow Liverpool supporter I know who spots me will often unload his latest thoughts and news about the team, even if I am deeply engrossed in a book that I keep trying to return to. It seems kind of baffling that someone would keep talking to someone who is reading a book, not least because possibly not a word they say will be heard.

A lady was coughing in a shop a few days ago and I asked what ailed her. It was like a torrent that I unleashed. The speed she started chronicling her medical history made it quite clear that she had a vast amount to describe. Far too much and far too intense in response to a casual inquiry. But it is a risk I take, and one I will keep taking. Besides, I did feel sorry for her as she clearly had had a rough time. But there is a kind of cardinal rule when talking with strangers to check that they remain conscious.

I was.

Just.

Rona and the Norwegian Ladies team

Back to the Homeless World Cup!

I had a mission to photograph the Pakistan team, but first wanted to watch South Africa men against Norway men. I climbed to the top of the stand and sat next to the Norwegian ladies team! Such is the nature of this event. The community spirit born out of a removal of status, and a removal of hierarchy. I chatted at length with the goalkeeper who had an impressive tattoo on one side of her face. She told me the nature of the tattoo art but I cannot recall. It did contain Celtic strands though, she confirmed.

Her name is called **Rona** and she is nearest to the camera in the photograph on the next page.

It transpired that this lively, warm, pretty-eyed lady, relaxed in conversation was like myself a sufferer of anxiety. **Rona** described how she can be drawn inwards and hide, or push outwards and ignore her feelings to expand into the world. Proof, yet again, that appearances very much are poor exhibitions of inner nature. (I later took videos and stills that I hope to send to her). Her son is profoundly autistic and had to be held in an institution because the meltdowns were too extreme for her and her partner to handle.

I later talked with a couple of Welsh families and the coach for the Dutch team (he grew up in raptures about their famous 'Total football', and of course Johann Cruyff).

The Pakistan team arrived to play against Hong Kong, and in their number was a friend I played football with at the local recreation field here in Cardiff. This was a little baffling as I had always assumed he was from an African country. But he played in the game nevertheless. Except that he left the field early with a twisted knee injury. The poor fellow. I managed to get some decent photographs that I will send to that president.

On the bus home I faced a father and his two children. One was reading a book so we talked about books. The father asked if I was a writer and it transpired that he writes short stories. I gave a copy of "Balancing Act" to the girl who also writes mystery stories. My book is a kind of mystery story, but not of the conventional type.

At the back of the bus was a group of boisterous young people. The boy in the middle had such an animated face that I told him so. Then the girl next to him started laughing.

A lot.

And it became like the sound of a hyena.

Which is what I impulsively blurted out, to much mirth, fortunately. But she was sooooooo happy in the laughing fit. She was so wonderfully connected with these boys. A genuine delight to behold. I would *love* to have captured that scene with my camera, but again it was not appropriate.

AUG 1 Boyd Clack

I was lured back to the World Cup football, not least to give **Rona** the url of the web site where I uploaded her photos.

As I waited for a bus, **Boyd Clack**'s face appeared out of nowhere :

This well respected actor and writer (The "Satellite City" TV series was his most famous creation) was in fine fettle, normally weighed down heavily by chronic depression, the poor man. We have chatted briefly over the years when bumping into each other in coffee shops or in the street. I mentioned to him that a fellow actor, Michael Sheen, had injected a lot of his life savings into the Homeless World Cup. His face lit up with respect for a fellow actor he placed in high regard.

At the football, I sat with a Norwegian man I met a few days ago watching the Norwegian Ladies play. To the left were raucous Belgiums, singing in French and, curiously, in English, and the Norwegians on my right trying, but failing, to out-sing them in Norwegian. They specifically cheered only the name of just one player – **Rona** – which I found odd.

At half time, she changed into an outfield kit so that she could play out of goal in the second half. I have never see a lady footballer (facing the pitch, not us) first remove her shirt and change it then her shorts to change them. Alas, her team were easily beaten again.

AUG 2   A few people

An even sunnier day, but I decided to take a break from the World Cup Football. In the afternoon, I walked to Waterloo tea shop (yet) again and sat outside with a University lecturer who additionally writes history books. One on the history of Catholicism in England, where uptake was rather oppressed in past times, and another on the history of Checkoslovakia. The first of these lead to discussions about religion, and her pet subject : the failure of religions in general to deal with the matter of suffering. That this was a consequence of being endowed with free will she saw as a thin argument. Myself also – if God is present when a child is abused by an adult, then surely this is not a fault of the child exercising free will?

After finishing my Jasmine Green tea, I bade her farewell and set off to sit in the park. Such an adherence to routine reflects my likely Aspergic nature, where the comfort of habit limits sensory and mental overload. But it felt terribly shallow to follow my routine today, in spite of the glorious sun and warm air, because it lacked the excitement and connectivity of the World Cup football. I felt that being spoilt with such riches was like a poisoned chalice – the richer the spectacle, the less appealing the simple things in life – including meditation – become. My mind wanted to compare sitting in the park with 'what I was missing' even though I plan to return for the finals day tomorrow. I chose to let that comparison voice fade and later moved seat from the shade to one in the sun. As I approached a park bench, I passed three ladies in black head-to-foot clothing having a picnic on the grass. I said to them "Good afternoon ladies" and was a little disappointed that this seemed to solicit no response (I think I simply did not hear).

But shortly after sitting down, one of the ladies approached me in a rather gingerly manner. As she neared, I could see her radiate the most wonderful, sweet smile. Her face was lit up as she offered me a complete Arabic meal on a plate. Sadly, I had not long eaten so declined, hoping this would not offend. (I decided that taking the food away to eat later felt wrong). After she returned to her seat I went over to the ladies and thanked her again. She said that she was from Iraq, and that made sense as the people from this country seem to connect and smile a great deal. The way in which Iraq has been portrayed by the media rarely shows that warmth.

AUG 5 — Sam the playwright

After my early morning gym session, I found myself ensconced with a boisterous man and his care worker in the coffee shop. It was a little too intense, so when the sun came out, I went to sit in the garden where I chatted with two new people, one leaving shortly before the other arrived. Yet it was not until an hour or so later that it occurred to me that I might write about them here. Sometimes, you see, I really do just get drawn into engaging with new people without any real agenda beyond that instinct for exploration and connection.

The first person was a tall, wiry man called **Sam** in super colourful trousers, black T-shirt and long wavy black hair. He could easily have been the bass guitarist in Black Sabbath. So I asked him if he was a musician. I was not terribly far wrong as he was an actor. And a playwright. And very easy to talk to. Somehow or other I got to talking about the splendid Pressberger and Powell film production "A matter of life and death" with Jack Cardiff on camera. I also enthused about "Somewhere in time", a time travel film revolving around playwrights. My mind jumps fast to such memories. Word association (football).

He was happy to read "Balancing Act" and let me know his thoughts. I am particularly keen to hear a playwright's considerations. Shortly after he left, a lady and the fluffiest of dogs came into the garden, followed by **Debbie**, one of the staff, with free chewy sausage to give to the canine. The lady (whose name I forgot to ask) was studying ancient religions. As far back as 5,000 years B.C., the time of the Sumerians. I necessarily asked her how she found the books to read, only to discover that she had to learn ancient languages in order to read them. And that she now has a scholarship in Lyon, France to continue her studies and research.

My sister Alison emigrated to Lyon some ten years or so ago!

AUG 6 · Some elderly gentlemen

When I returned to the main counter in the shop to get a tea refill in my morning tea-drinking session, I found myself standing next to a tall, slender vision of a beauty. As if I had set foot on a James Bond set.

It is pretty easy to speak to such beauties when you are past a certain age as they no longer see you as a threat to fend off. At least I think this is the case. This wonderfully pretty lady, with beauty yet again enhanced by a smile, and markedly high cheekbones was from Moscow. Which is precisely where the daughter, **Tiffany** of my sister **Alison** emigrated from France to.

It was a coffee shop double today, as the clouds cleared in the afternoon to make a trip to Waterloo tea shop highly desirable. I still run half a dozen web sites and had just fixed a web site transfer problem which put me into an upbeat mood. I sat outside under interleaving sun and cloud reading a my book about the healing affect of the sun. I had no idea at all how deep the sun on skin effect went. It is clearly rather more than a matter of burn, cancer and vitamin D. It also actually serves to provide protection against a number of cancers. That might surprise a lot of people.

After a while, a group of elderly and rather slow-walking gentleman, very smartly dressed, edged ever so slowly into the cafe. I remarked to one that his hair was wonderfully white, and that I was waiting for my grey hair to do the same. He declared that he had turned white aged seven. He knew of nothing that might have triggered that change.

It was then that it occurred to me that this man's voice was very familiar. I realised that he sounded uncannily like **Boyd Clack**. He told me that his name was **Ray** and amazingly that he lives in the house opposite **Boyd Clack**. He told me to mention his name to **Boyd** the next time I see him.

You might feel inclined to declare me a fraud. That such coincidences as this really are not likely to happen in daily life at the rate that they are happening to me. But this is precisely what happened.

Afterwards, I spoke with a young man opposite me who was reading a book about Chinese maltreatment of Christians. We talked about synchronicity – describing his own Christian form of this concept. **Joe** said that he may choose the paths in each day – to do this then that – but that God would guide his feet so that the right things happened. God filled in the details, as it were, sometimes creating synchronicities. This piqued my interest. It seemed a more subtle take on God's role. I mentioned **Talia** to him and it reminded me that I miss talking with her. It would seem that she has returned to Cheddar and her family. But I strongly suspect that we will chat again one day.

AUG 12 Jayde

I sat near the back of the bus on my way home from town. In the seats immediately in front of me were a lady and what I presumed to be her young daughter.

They were going to the hospital so I asked if they were paying a visit to someone in the hospital. The lady was happy to chat, and that no, she was a child-minder taking the girl to her home in the Heath. I mentioned that my parents used to live in the Heath and we chatted a while on the back of that.

Jayde was a delight. Very open and receptive – the little girl quiet and wary by contrast. **Jayde** declared that she loved her job, and was always happiest in the company of children. It was easy to sense this.

A very giving, caring lady.

AUG 13 Cyber security business startup CEO

A day blessed with plenty of sunshine urged me to travel by bus not just to get somewhere, but also as a means of enjoying meditations on the illuminated scenery gliding past. A simple pleasure that many of those wedded to their phones will be incapable of enjoying as their threshold for novelty has been hammered. The bus took me to Pontypridd again. And on the next page you can see the wonderful park full of children playing.

I sat on a bench near the park and started to mix reading with sunbathing and meditation. Yes, yes, yes, I am very much aware that this is a luxurious life. A life of old Riley. The freedom to largely do as I please (subject to mental health issues though – I sat there with a headache that lasted into

the evening). But having acquired the headache, the intense chat I was about to have next was at least not to be blamed for instigating a headache – the 'damage' was already done, as it were.

The man I talked with, or more correctly, listened to, was most fascinating, and notably different in personality from myself. **Michael Whitlock** was a former top IBM salesman, now deeply, and clearly passionately involved in setting up a cyber-security business. He 'sold me' the extremeness of his idea with the enthusiasm and energy of a young man. He had highly talented men working for him (of course) and even had contact with an FBI cyber-threat expert.

Fortunately, we also talked about politics, so there was some common ground – some dialogue. But only to the point where we had to beg to differ, he as far right-wing as I am left-wing. He declared Jeremy Corbyn, the labour leader to be as 'nutty as a fruitcake' and that a Labour government would be an economic disaster. And all this intensity and energy was emanating from a *seventy-four* year old man!

Michael

A few weeks ago, I watched one of the older juniors being coached at the tennis club at the end of my road. Clearly he was thinking very much about shot placement, in contrast with the more sledgehammer or mechanical methods of most juniors. But this seventeen year old, **Lorca**, was very shy, rarely chatting with anyone, and not making himself available for any of the teams.

So I challenged him on his reluctance to chat with other players at the social tennis mixed doubles sessions. His response then was to say that some people can be quiet and should be allowed to be so. I necessarily had to agree.

This evening at the social doubles session, possibly because I had tried to connect with him, he actually sat with me and instigated some chat. Somehow or other, we got talking about maths and computer programming. I did not know that these subjects are pretty much all that interest him. He said that it was crazy that no one had told him that I could be someone to talk to about them. I mentioned the famous book "Godel, Escher, Bach: An Eternal Golden Braid" by Hofstadter that links mathematics to art and music, but one I struggled to comprehend. He became animated and declared that he had read and loved it.

Having thus connected, we were then unexpectedly allowed to connect in a very different way as we were asked to play our tennis championships 'consolation' singles match. It proved to be a great contest, the stroke making and shot choice a meeting of thinking minds. He won in a third set tie-break. I limped home exhausted and with very sore knees ...

AUG 14 — Scott on the KGS Go game server

I sometimes encounter friendly people playing games of Go on the KGS Go Server. Sadly, most who play the game seem to be bluntly unsociable. I guess that many want to focus on play without distracting dialogue with a stranger. As you probably surmised, I find that chat enhances play. Often when I do try to converse with an opponent, however, opponents tell me off, saying that they are there only to play. It feels like they are playing a bot, not a human, showing a chilling disinterest in connecting with others.

But one player that I have played a number of games with recently has been a delight to pit my wits with and converse with. **Scott** is a Scott, living a few hundred miles north of Cardiff. Always polite and gracious, he studies *Zazen*, a seated form of meditation. When I told him about this book, he said that he had a synchronicity to share with me! Or rather, he had a number, and this was his favourite. I offer it in his own words, verbatim :

Around fifteen years ago my wife and I came into a little bit of money when her old mum who had come to live with us was able to sell her house. It was decided that I would use some to try getting a photography business off the ground, and the first requisite was a vehicle. We decided a Land Rover would be best, considering the kind of places I would most often want to visit to take photographs. I started looking around and found literally hundreds all over the country, and chose first to go and look at one relatively nearby, an hour's drive away. It was being sold by an old lady whose husband had died. It was in great condition and at a sensible price so we decided to have it. With it, the old lady kindly provided a lot of spares and tools etc., and a big wooden crate full of dozens of copies of Land Rover Owner magazine.

I should explain at this point that my wife's mum's name was Marjorie King, and that she intensely disliked it all her life when people spelled it wrong, as Marjory or, even worse, Margerie.

A day or two after taking the Landy home, and excited at the next step of having signage put on it reading "Eden Photographic", I decided to have a look at some of the old magazines, and chose one at random. There must have been sixty or maybe eighty copies, a huge stack: this was the first one I had looked at. After reading for five or ten minutes I turned the page and saw, as part of a Readers' Mail page, a small photograph of an old Land Rover standing in countryside. On its side was affixed a sign, which to my astonishment read "Marjorie King Photographic". The fact that her name was even spelled correctly was the icing on the great cake of coincidence.

The number of vehicles to choose from, multiplied by the number of magazines, multiplied by the number of versions of the old lady's name, multiplied by the number of types of business in which the truck in the photo might have been involved, must be astronomical. Even dear old Marjorie, after several strokes, was able to muster a show of great surprise. I still have the photograph!

AUG 16   Ripple eco-friendly shop

Yesterday, I visited a most splendid shop called *Ripple* some three minutes away from my home. My first visit for a number of weeks. It is an ethically-minded shop, dispensing all sorts of beans and pulses from large containers into paper bags. Not a plastic bag to be seen anywhere. And bulk purchases without discrete packaging allows them to sell at low prices. So the three bags of lentils and bag of split-peas came to just £1.05. A 'billy bargain' as we say in some parts of the UK. I later cooked and ate some of the lentils with avocado and a mixed salad.

Today the rains set in. But mid afternoon, with the notion of being ensconced at home holding too little charm, I set on foot to a tea shop half way up a hill. My first time there. There was a window seat with one of three chairs already occupied. I briefly spoke with the occupant of the first seat who was doing dull accounts, but who liked to sit and gaze at the rain from time to time as it reminded her of camping. I read in turn from each of the three books I had bought with me whilst drinking a latte claimed to be large but clearly confounding that description. Tasty but petit.

Before leaving I asked the lady if she would get time to relax today and if the accounts were for a business. They were. And it transpired that **Sophie** owns the Ripple shop I went to yesterday.

This was one of her rare escapes from the shop where she finds it easier to do the dull part of the business. The paper-work, or pixel-work as it were. But she was happy to chat a while, saying that her business was not-for-profit and she managed it alone. It was flourishing, and for good reason. She was given lots of advice of how to expand, but was principally thinking about how to help others to do as she did. But not the franchise idea, she made a point of saying. Indeed, business advisers struggled to understand the not-for-profit, ethical nature of her motives. She had formerly been a journalist for an ethical magazine, the concepts presumably catalysing this venture.

She was energised and delightful to talk to. She recommended that I explore the spices she has in store, and hearing this from her means that this is not a business push but a sharing notion.

AUG 17 — Pushing Bob in his motorised wheelchair

I rushed from coffee with my sister to get to the tennis club to watch the start of the club championships finals. On my way, a man I have often seen 'driving' his one-seat motorised support vehicle along the road was this time stationary and seeking my intention. "Can you push me a bit – my battery is dead" he asked.

This was the first time this happened to him, he said. I asked what he would do after I pushed him a bit. He was not sure. So I pushed him home – about a third of a mile. It was surprisingly tiring on my legs, but there again, it was also good exercise. It was a situation that would frequently have seen me become very irritable in the past – in a rush and taking forever in a distraction. But I decided to ignore that schedule and get stuck into this vehicular pushing as if it were my job. Besides, the club matches would last hours!

Bob is a friendly fellow. He had use of his legs, but after about a hundred yards, they would get extremely tired or sore. Hence the transport. He ran a business, surprisingly selling truck tyres. When he eased his body out of the vehicle, a 'builders cleavage' was presented to me. He was most happy to have been assisted and I went on my way feeling happy to have helped.

AUG 18 — Sunday morning coffee shop meeting with people

Being a regular at the same coffee house offers a kind of yin and yang set of experiences. I meet lots of people, making many friends, but some days I cannot sit in peace because there are so many to talk with. A kind of pretty benign problem, however, of course.

Today I asked a young man if I could sit in the comfy chair next to him. The chair facing the sun through the large window that I hog an unreasonable amount. He was instantly comfortable chatting with me. A shop-fitter by trade, **Osman** could clearly out-talk and out-interrupt me. That is no mean feat. He said I looked fit and healthy and why was I not looking for a partner. I replied that I needed too much time alone, and changed the subject to sport to say that I still played tennis. So he asked for a hit as he was in the process of joining the tennis club I belong to. We tentatively arranged for him to join me in with my 'rally with Sally' in the afternoon.

As we chatted, **Connie** and **Dean** came through the door and said hello. They are somewhat older than I but have been together since they were both fourteen. A lovely, giving couple. And then **Caroline** appeared through the door – I had not seen her and her friend **Sandra** in months, so I later popped over to talk with them. Quite a long catchup chat.

On the next table was a mother and daughter I see from time to time. The mother quite elderly but as elegant as her daughter who works in medicine I believe. When they later left the shop, they chatted at length whilst standing outside the shop, the window then open as I sat in the comfy chair, basking in the sun.

The two families I see most Sundays then also appeared. The three children popped back and forth to show me drawings they had done. **Jude** and **Martha** both gave me a drawing, but somehow or other I chose only to do a flower drawing in return for **Mabel,** who was so thrilled she came back to sit on my lap for maybe as long as five minutes. Mum and dad came over and we chatted. **Mabel** every so often just hugged me.

Such affection was most delightful and endearing but I also felt quite uncomfortable as society frowns so heavily on non-family members being this close to children. But I adore and respect children deeply. This is where another fear comes from I think. Not wanting to do anything that might fracture this affectionate connection. I was most tired after all this. But it was a very rich hour or so, and tiredness is a kind of collateral.

AUG 19 Salamander limb regeneration

The book on the healing effect of sunlight lead me to a book on electromagnetism in the human body – "The Body Electric" (Becker and Selden) written in 1985, but wonderful and relevant reading so far. A rare author able to articulate ideas with such clarity is this :

> *"Too many physicians no longer learn from their patients, only from their professors. The breakthroughs against infections convinced the profession of its own infallibility and quickly ossified its beliefs into dogma. Life processes that were inexplicable according to current biochemistry have been either ignored or misinterpreted. In effect, scientific medicine abandoned the central rule of science – revision in light of new data."*

The book starts with the ability of creatures like hydra to regrow severed parts, and in particular Salamanders, being vertebrates topologically similar to us, explaining how this ability transferred to humans in some small fashion but has inexplicably been overlooked by the medical profession.

AUG 23   Tamsin again

Whilst sat in the comfy, window-facing chair in Coffee #1 this morning, an elderly lady with walking stick plumped herself down in the adjacent chair without a word spoken. She proceeded to tell of the premature death of her mother, and that no less than three hundred people had turned up for the funeral. But I was reading my book, kept returning to my book, and still she talked on. I did not mind so much as she was getting a little tearful and declared that she could not talk of her mother to everyone. But when I eventually left she said "You do not like my company?". I just repeated that it was time for me to go. But no, I was not enjoying her company as she had engaged in a monologue with barely a pause to try to connect with me. I was, it felt, merely someone to offload worries upon. It was OK though, in one sense, since it was of value to her to be heard.

But truth is that I am also connecting less with people the past week or so. I am projecting less – not feeling an openness to others. This is not good. So I probably need to stop being too self-absorbed, a state easy to slide back into. It may be, however, how deeply enthralled I have been in the "Body Electric" book I am now reading. Did you know that removing half the heart of a newt, then closing up the body, the heart will regenerate enough within just four hours to start beating again? Why can they not tell us such fascinating facts in school?

I received an email today promoting a single book (even though the text refers to 'these items'). Normally, emails promote multiple books. The book being promoted was most certainly not the result of a search on Amazon. So it is all the more puzzling that it should be this book :

93

This was a particularly hot and sunny late August day, so I later walked to Waterloo gardens and tea shop. I was delighted to see **Tamsin** and her mother sat outside. So I sat at the other table and chatted. She was more subdued than before, but still articulated with passion and pace.

She explained that she had an auto-immune system problem now, where her processing of Vitamin B12 was malfunctioning. So she had to have weekly intravenous injections, and they created a drowsiness, a fogginess, something that I could readily relate to. As ever, she researched her condition with intense enthusiasm, and related to me what she had found. Clearly, this is a lady who could readily teach medicine, and do so in a way that inculcated understanding. (Her dyslexia, however, made the use of technical terms rather a struggle). From her research she found that celery juice – a full sixteen fluid ounces of it – instead of breakfast would clear that fogginess. She tried this for a week and the effect was profound. It also assuaged the hunger she normally had after waking.

She also has had another condition, where her inner ear became infected. Fortunately it does not lead to vertigo. But it requires an operation. And like me, she is waiting endless months for that to happen.

Her mother was having a break in an eighteen hour working day. She cannot take her employers to a tribunal on such a matter as she would likely lose her job. So the abuse of care workers carries on, casually, but in a clearly callously exploitative manner at times. It was a delight to chat with them on this sunny day. This time I was not overly tired afterwards. I hope it is not so long next time before I bump into this family again.

AUG 27 Serif Affinity

After my early morning gym session, I had my customary pots of tea in Coffee #1, but sat in the conservatory at the back for a change. An architect had drawings sprawled across the table he was working at but was wonderfully open for a little chat. I took the opportunity to talk about transmission of sunlight, or accommodation of sun in modern buildings. He said that many commercial designs rarely embraced such a matter, but the occasional 'bespoke' building contract did.

After his departure, a mother and daughter sat on the next table from me. The mother was most excited and energised in her conversation after I found reason to talk – I asked about the triangle motif on her t-shirt. I should have recognised it as the logo of the Serif Affinity suite of publishing software. The husband of this British resident French lady, it transpires, creates tutorial videos for this product line. I have used Serif PagePlus in the past to write books and now use Serif Affinity Publisher to create this book. Not sure there can be many people sporting such a T-shirt.

AUG 28 Talking on the bus

A grey day with hints of blue sky and sunshine. But surprisingly enjoyable being transported home by bus. A rather full bus, so the young lady entering at one point had no choice but to ask to sit next to me. She was blonde with a particularly gentle face. And she was entirely happy to chat, on her way to a menial job in the city centre.

So I asked her, as I often do in such situations, what job she would love to do if she could choose. She declared that she would love to work in a school with young children that have special needs. As she spoke, she smiled and her face became even more gentle, exuding a natural humility and humbleness. She said that she was not smart but I pointed out that there were many forms of smart, not least social and emotional.

The lady in front had overheard our conversation, and apologised for interrupting, but felt compelled to say that she works in a school with special needs children, and made a good point that across Cardiff they were often in need of new staff to help.

I left the two of then chatting when I disembarked. As I walked away from the bus stop, the young lady waved goodbye and I felt that if I should see her again I should make a point of telling her how delightful she was to talk with. As I have probably repeated saying in similar situations before, her warmth of nature amplified her beauty.

AUG 29 Unable to chat

In Coffee #1 afterwards, I asked if I could sit in the comfy chair adjacent a lady reading a magazine. I tried twice, very briefly, to engage in conversation with her and it was clear she was not interested.

But she was intriguing to me! I wanted to chat because the way she spoke was quite different from most people I meet. She had a kind of unaffected nature, untarnished or normalised convention. But I let her be. I try to make a point of respecting privacy as much as I can.

AUG 30 A Chinese lady called Susan

The gentleman I joined this morning in Coffee #1 was particularly strong of mind. Quite forceful, so it was no surprise that he was against Labour, inappropriately finding reason to criticise them. Always, it seems, bullish, strident people have reason to attack Labour – even though doing so is essentially attacking a force for social good. I tensed up with a bit of a headache, but enjoyed the challenge of chatting amicably whilst not agreeing. He took to that very well also, and we found some common political ground, not least the benefit that would be accrued from replacing all MPs with a new batch. But he did not agree that it was a systemic problem, and that Westminster was too attractive and exploitable by self-serving, careerist politicians. It is the asylum, not the inmates, that is the key problem.

Early afternoon I set off on a walk around the lake. The sun flitted in and out of clouds in a most pleasant manner. I was carrying a new book in my rucksack, about the first lady, Henrietta Lacks, who was able to 'provide' a supply of cancer cells that rapidly multiplied outside of her body in a laboratory petri dish. None had done so before. This was deeply profound because her harvested cells, and their offspring have been a boon to medicine and science and continue to be so, yet the lady and her family received no gain from this, in part because of the colour of her skin.

Before I resumed reading it whilst sat on a bench in Roath Park I greeted a Chinese lady walking past. She eventually sat down and we chatted for maybe half an hour. We were like peas in a pod. She too talked with strangers, but was disappointed by how few here in Cardiff return greetings or stop to chat. She was around my age, a great and empathic talker. And an enigma – she challenged me to guess the subject she lectured in at University. I tried but used up my three guesses. I was to try again next time I saw her as she is a regular walker around the lake. Daily, in fact. Her adopted English name is **Susan**, the same as my ex-wife. She had three published books but would not tell me about them as it would reveal her subject.

I offered her one of my books, but she declined, preferring to take up the offer later after she had had cataract operations performed. She was fascinated to learn about fasting, however, and the value of fat in the diet, subjects I was more than happy to evangelise about.

Walking back through the rose gardens, I beheld a wondrous site. A dog nearly the size of a small horse, with a lady and her two granddaughters sat on a bench behind it. We talked for maybe twenty minutes, the youngest girl barely allowing her elder sister time to get a word in edgeways. So I made a point of listening to her. The grandmother was a retired history teacher.

Both chats had aggravated my head – I was literally straining. This is upsetting, or would be if I let it. The joy of the chats was my focus and easily worth the strain.

Friends were playing tennis in the evening so I sat on a bench facing the court. After a while, I felt compelled to lie back, head on my book, and meditate on the cloudscape above. Oh boy, it was magnificent! Multi-layered, with a blue backdrop speckled with cloudettes, and swathes of cotton wool rushing past in the foreground. Deeply relaxing, the act of facing upwards making the sky the sole sight for me to behold. It is much easier to see life anew when experienced from a different perspective.

AUG 31 Graham

Another sun-flecked afternoon, another coffee shop. Again, I barely started to read my book before engaging in conversation with the gentleman who decided to sit at my table outside. A very *gentle* man, in fact, articulate and smart, going by the name of **Graham**. We eventually talked about Aspergers and the Government's callous and calculated mistreatment of disabled benefits claimants. And he was able to talk with some authority on the amateurish way that the Department for Work and Pensions handled PIP (Personal Independence Payments) for disabled people because he worked in this field. Additionally, his son has Aspergers.

I could not always easily understand what **Graham** said as he had a speech impediment, his mouth slurring the words against his will. It was a delight to avoid the stigma of presuming that the inability to articulate sounds was a reflection of a matching inability to articulate ideas. Clearly, I was in the presence of a smarter man than I. Or maybe a wiser one. Not too sure which.

When he bade farewell, I returned to reading about Henrietta Lacks. The narrative was describing the cervical cancer that afflicted this poor woman back in 1951. There were two recognised types of cervical cancer, with the version she had described as being *in situ* – Latin for being in the original place. A surface cancer that experts presumed did not need aggressive treatment. Necessarily, Henrietta did not get the aggressive treatment she really actually needed and consequently did not live long.

My point in mentioning this is that whenever I encounter Latin words and expressions, they feel terribly familiar. It is hard to express this feeling, but it is as if I have always been deeply imbued with the language. Yet I have never studied or been taught it. And I typically immensely struggle with the acquisition of the words of any language but English. But my father was au fait with that language, able to give the Latin names of all the plants in his garden.

Somehow, maybe I acquired some of that understanding without explicitly or knowingly doing so. The matter remains a mystery but a sweet one, each time the inexplicable wave of familiarity with words that should be alien appears, I get a frisson of delight.

SEP 1 — An Aspergic couple

Sunday morning and there is the most wondrous image in front of me in the coffee shop. I am pretty certain she is the most colourfully dressed lady I have ever encountered. Vivid, saturated colours in her top, pastel colours in hat and trousers. Even more, her eye-liners sported an array of bright colours, with a sprinkling of gold dust on her cheeks. Naturally, I had to proclaim to her how wonderful she looked.

Jess and her companion **Josh** turned out to both be Aspergic, yet flamboyantly clothed as if seasoned extroverts about to go on stage. They were gentle in nature and lovely to talk with. She is also an artist, like myself (although I am more a *former* artist I have to admit). **Jess** showed me on her phone some of her (many) paintings. The colours were as scintillating as her clothing. Almost naive in style, they really did look wonderful, vivid of colour and expression as far as the little thumbnails could reveal.

I have always endorsed saturated colours in art – pastel seems too often to be a flawed, limited compromise, a kind of denial of the possible. She also showed me an amazingly realistic drawing she had done of one of her relatives. Clearly, she is technically gifted as well as aesthetically so. I gave them a draft copy of this book to read and (hopefully) feed back. It may be that they were relatively shy, so it might be enlightening to hear of a similarly Aspergic introvert talking with strangers.

I was itching to ask to photograph **Jess**. But it felt wrong. Clearly not so wrong, though, as she said they were actually setting off to be photographed.

Frankie on Instagram

Coffee #1 and no seats in the sun to be had anywhere. Doh! Upstairs I came across a frowning **Talia**, working at her laptop. It was great to see her again. She looked as calm, beautiful and serene as ever, in spite of her focus of attention. I said to her that I preferred to talk with her face to face rather than electronically as the former is so much more meaningful. She agreed.

But it was very noisy upstairs so I bade my farewell after that brief chat and ventured downstairs and out into the garden. As I passed a lady reading in the conservatory I stopped to ask her about the book she was absorbed in.

She said that it was a novel from her childhood that she was returning to. These words she spoke were delivered with the most wondrous smile. I told her how nice she smiled, never seeming to tire of saying that. I asked if she was a keen reader. When she declared that she was indeed an avid reader, I gave her a copy of "Balancing Act".

I eventually found my way to the comfy chair in the window, immediately opened the window 'doors' and basked in the warm sun. After a while, **Talia** appeared on her way out of the cafe, and we had a longer chat. This was delightful. We were both more relaxed than in the mayhem upstairs.

At one point, she said that she had discovered that I had made an appearance on *Instagram*. Or to be more precise, a photo of my book and nice words had appeared. The lady I had given the book to a little while earlier turned out to be **Frankie**, one of Talia's Christian friends.

It is indeed a small world. **Frankie** told Talia that she was excited to get the book as it kind of restored her faith in humanity – that some stranger can give with no sign of seeking to receive back.

It is easy for me to give, so it is not something particularly special that I do. Besides, I find it really nice to share the thoughts and ideas that I have expressed in my books.

Little did I know that a short book such as mine was a welcome addition to the hundred book reading project she was undertaking.

The boy in the window

As I passed a boy in the park on my way to Waterloo tea shop, we both said hello to each other. I am not sure who spoke first. When I found my seat outside, I turned around to discover that he was inside, waving back to me. I went inside and spoke with his mother who said that he was indeed a most sociable fellow. He is in the picture below. I sat with my pot of tea to read further in (yet) another new book entitled "Inner Story" about the unconscious stories that guide how we behave without us being terribly aware of these guiding forces.

7 Email from Ana

It has been a long time since I heard from my Spanish friend Ana. The last email was maybe a couple of weeks ago. So I sent her an email asking if all is OK. I was a bit concerned. I am not normally good at that – at tracking the welfare of others.

Instantly after I sent that email, a new email appeared in my mailbox. From **Ana**.

Crazy precision of timing!

8 The most delightful family

I have not long since returned from an hour sat in the garden of Cameo restaurant in Wellfield Road. The last rays of warm sun bathed the garden. As I took my seat, I started what was to be a long chat with the most enchanting family you could care to meet. **Suzanne** was my principle point of contact, although I also talked at length with her husband **Leon**. They had two boys and two girls, exactly as for my childhood, something that is not particularly common.

She was so totally accepting of whatever way I spoke with her and whatever I spoke about. It felt at any moment she would revert to be like most people and become defensive, or patronise but not really connect with me. But she and I remained engaged in spirited conversation, largely about art because one of her children was very artistic and she herself had been on a course. She showed me some of her art and it was genuinely very good. But she was not sure yet if she had found her niche. She said that next time we meet she will be sure to have more art to show me.

Their four children were sat with them eating. Or to be more precise, three of the four children were. **Jasmine**, the artistic one, refused to eat, and was not in a good place emotionally.

I had a great chat with **Leon** about health prevention, his former job, and the state of politics, where Boris Johnson is currently enduring the worst start to any Prime Ministerial career imaginable.

Suzanne and **Leon** were wonderfully easy going, as were three of the children, who seemed ludicrously happy of disposition. Their three year old boy soon came over to me to show me his *Where's Wally?* books. He held my hand as he did so, pretty devoid of any fear of strangers. The other girl (I only remember **Jasmine's** name, alas) eventually came to talk to me face to face whilst sporting a big grin.

But I preferred to place my attention on **Jasmine** who seemed all at odds with her siblings. I wanted her to see that her endless passion for art was in part reason for her emotional sensitivity. Or the other way around. When later they left, she was in tears and I tried to console her as best I could. **Suzanne** works with disadvantaged children so seemed to fully understood my efforts.

The deep engagement with this family reminded me of the way Liverpudlians make you feel completely relaxed. I left for home feeling a profound sense of contentment. This is very rare for me. A kind of *reset*.

SEP 9 Bumping into Boyd

After a harrowing morning seeing a surgeon in Llandough hospital regarding my bad knee, my routine was thrown out of kilter. So I supped my English Breakfast tea in the middle of the afternoon at Coffee #1 rather than as a part of my normal early morning routine. After a while, **Boyd Clack** appeared in tow behind his wife. So I jumped at the chance of telling him about his friend **Ray**, which brought a grin to his face.

After explaining about this book, I told him another story from it, and described these things as synchronicities, which lit up his face as he had a story of his own from a few years ago to tell.

His colleague, John, decided to take a mini-break and head off for a ramble in the Highlands of Scotland. A break from routine. One day, he was passing a telephone box, in the days where they were still used. As he did so, the phone rang.

Curious, he entered the box and picked up the receiver.

The voice asked "Is that John?"

It was a call from work! Apparently, they had typed a single digit incorrectly and were routed to this box rather than his home landline phone.

He later told me that he had been asked to stand for a political role in *Plaid Cymru* (a social democratic independent Welsh party). He was bemused by this notion, and clearly was thinking in depth about it. His principle concerns were about his chequered past. My point to him was that he might be too honest. He agreed. But I said that it would be a fascinating thing for him to try – maybe to get inside-stories as seeds for a new television script.

SEP 10 A cascade of chats

To Coffee #1 after a workout in the gym. I was lucky, again, to get the comfy chair facing the pavement and sunshine. With these tales of constant coffee shop trips, maybe you can see that the novelty wears off after a while. I would prefer to be able to work without getting headaches than go to coffee shops each day. I miss the repartee and the sense of communal purpose.

Today I had acquired a mild headache after a ludicrously short chat with **Kieran** in the gym so wanted to relax and read. I did some of this, but most of the two and a half hours I spent there I was chatting. Quite tiring, but an elevating distraction from discomfort.

A lady by the name of **Irene** sat down in the adjacent chair after about forty-five minutes. An articulate and lively seventy-eight year old with no less than six great-grandchildren. She was fascinating to talk with because of her lucid and entertaining manner as well as an interesting life to relate. She declared that she was blessed, in her words, not with any skill or talent, but with a calm pragmatism about life and a cheerful disposition. This meant that no less than thirty years spent nursing her poorly but deeply loved husband was never seen as a burden. But it did spur her to travel a lot in the following years as a form of catchup. It was, however, a bit of a struggle now as her hip bone osteoarthritis became so bad that the bone had actually merged with her femur.

Not long after she left, **Malcolm** appeared for a chat. Not a particularly special dialogue this time, and unexpectedly cut short by the appearance of **Talia**. She launched into a story about flat hunting, and **Malcom** quietly took his leave.

She seemed different this time, and part of my mind felt a little alienated. I hate this feeling. I see no value in it so I let it fade. But I suspect that my face showed some of it. I am, in a sense, not being authentic by harbouring and hiding such feelings, but am I really? I do not choose for these strange feelings to percolate up. They are momentary judgements that I do not want and therefore do not have to pay creed to. Fortunately, conversation was wonderful and became more animated than usual. She was stressed in a way that looked like 1% less than her normal calm. Amazing.

After a while, another person sat down in the chair next to me without invitation. Kind of reassuring that people feel they can do that. It was **Luca** who used to work in the Coffee #1 around the corner. He now took over the focal point in the dialogue, and **Talia** eventually drew up a seat to join us. It was a nice surprise to see **Luca** again as he is a most interesting and very authentic man who I had not spoken with for maybe a year or so.

His one year daughter was sat on his lap. **Feya** has transformed his life. Partying, drug taking and such reckless habits were now clearly seen as a relic of an ill-informed earlier lifestyle. He studies spiritualism now and is clearly beating a very different path through life. And he was most terribly excited by it.

In particular, he said that he connects with the universe and hears guiding voices. A very sane, grounded man is saying these things. What we personally do not experience we often do not truly understand, so I allowed for what he was saying.

And then he comes out with the *synchronicities* word. His very connected life now is replete with them. The story he told to us was rather involved, and very much as hard to believe as **Boyd**'s tale yesterday.

A girl he met up with recently asked him back to her house for coffee, I think he said. He asked her if her road was nearby. When she told him the street, he had to ask her the house number. And, as you probably guessed, it was where he had previously lived. But the story does not end there.

When they arrived, she rushed to take a book off the shelf for **Luca** to read. *The alchemist* by Paul Cohelco. A while later, he left to meet with Tom, an actor he had recently befriended who is guiding **Luca** into acting as a career. After greeting him, it appears that just as **Luca** was pulling out that book from his bag to show Tom, that Tom was also pulling out of his bag a book he had got from the library.

The alchemist.

Luca's honesty and openness seems to be facilitating such extreme synchronicities as this. But I became most tired and eventually bade them farewell. A series of chats that were simultaneously energising and tiring.

Rachel, fine artist

With the prospect of a clear blue sky in the afternoon, I had an early lunch before taking the 132 slow bus from outside Cardiff Castle to Pontypridd. It has been a while since I travelled in bright sunshine, which may explain why the trees and hills were mesmerising as they rushed past outside. Most certainly, after enough meditation, landscapes become enriched to the eye and emotion. The intermingling of leaves and sparkling bright sun was breathtaking.

After a walk to explore beyond the centre, I returned to indulge in a latte at the Costa Coffee franchise in the lower of the 'high' streets. But first I had to ask a lady sat outside if I could sit on one of the seats at her table in the sun. She obliged and proved to be wonderfully engaging company. Such an animated face and nature as you can see in the picture on the next page.

With a distinction in her Fine Art degree, she was shortly about to start a Masters degree in Fine Art with the theme of sleep and the unconscious. As we spoke, **Rachel** kind of bubbled over with a mix of curiosity and things to say. I think I intrigued her. Talking with her was a kind of adventure, as you could see her mind triggered with thoughts and feelings each step of the way. A face incapable of hiding feelings inside, it felt. So a complete stranger really did not feel aloof or distant whatsoever.

She asked me if I was still working, and then what I did when I had been working. When I said that I had written books on the game of Go, she declared that she plays the game with her husband who has his own Go set. In Britain, this is pretty rare. So I was pleasantly surprised. She took a copy of "Balancing Act" to read.

I blurted out at one point that I struggle to do abstract art as I cannot easily visualise. She immediately described this as *antaphasia* – the literal inability to form images in the mind. And she declared that she also has this condition, even though an artist. She actually travelled to meet with the originator of the term, *Adam Zeman*, to talk about the subject. From her perspective, she feels the condition is more widespread than the 2% rate generally cited. It certainly feels fairly normal to me. Sadly, she had to leave earlier than I would have liked. Such a mercurial lady.

I walked to the bus station just as the fast X4 bus to Cardiff was pulling out. Strange then that another should pull in one minute later. I had the whole bus to myself as far as the Cardiff outskirts. When showing my free bus pass, I asked the driver where her accent was from. All over, she declared.

Rachel

But there had to be some London in there, and yes, she said, she did live in Hackney at one point. When I said that I lived in Stoke Newington during my time working at the BBC, she said that she used to drive a bus there.

I nearly did not add this little 'factette' here because it seemed so ordinary. But it is another synchronicity.

SEP 15 — Rachel replies

I received emails from Rachel saying that she has already read the book I gave her and mostly liked it. She gave me some links to follow up on dreaming – and as a consequence I ordered a copy of "Dreams of Awakening" about lucid dreaming. She showed me drawings made by *Lee Hardin*, a man who literally draws in his sleep. During her dissertation, she met up with him in Cardiff to learn about his take on the nature of dreaming.

You see, I hope, that meeting others can open new areas of interest. Part *human-web* and part *planet-web* as I see it.

She also said this in her email :

> "*Thank you for talking to me the other day. I was feeling rather distracted.*
>
> *The sunshine is such a comfort isn't it?*"

SEP 16 — Anatomy of an epidemic

I often carry two or three books with me in my capacious backpack, but the past few days only one, so good is it. "Anatomy of an epidemic" is a fairly long, but cleverly well organised and researched exposure of flaws in the treatment of mental health conditions in the US.

By way of example, it explains that anti-psychotic drugs do not work as they should. They seek to decrease a presumed excess of dopamine. The brain reacts to the reduction by increasing dopamine receptor sensitivity. It seeks to fix the imbalance the drug is trying to create! When the patient stops taking the drug, normal dopamine levels resume and the increased sensitivity of receptors can then create a worse problem than was there in the first place. At least this is how I have understood the central theme of the book.

Before taking my seat in Waterloo tea shop to read, I spoke to a very friendly lady, **Laura**, from Northern Ireland. A viola player by profession, happy to read a draft copy of this book.

On my way home, I crossed paths with **Boyd Clack**. This time, I asked him what he was up to – was he working at present. He was happy to talk about a film he has a small part in. About the actress **Carol Hawkins** and her fight with *schizophrenia*. So I was well positioned to talk about this subject having just been reading about it!

Boyd raised a key point that the book has yet to cover, but which is of course absolutely vital to this debilitating mental health condition – if existing drugs are abandoned because of long term effects, what do you use in place of them? For many people, the short term benefits are so immense that long term 'side-effects' have to be tolerated.

I hope this subject matter is not too sad or tedious for you to read about. But if mental health issues are alien to you, be grateful – be very grateful as they can create a deep, deep spiral. One aspect that **Boyd** talked of most fiercely was that chronic depression for him was at root so *extremely boring*. He has a lively, sharp mind, so to be mindlessly dulled by depression, virtually forced to spend vast amounts of time in a lack-lustre, lifeless mental state that is by definition devoid of excitement, rhythm – of anything that can stir the soul – drives him crazy.

SEP 18 Sweet talking

The best way that I can describe the two chats with strangers that I had today is that were very sweet. On the front seat at the top of the double-decker bus into the city centre early afternoon, I again enjoyed the unfolding vista. As happens many times, I was sure that the bus could not turn in the tight spaces it often had to negotiate. But there were no bumps or scraping sounds.

To my left, a few seats away was a young lady assembling a roll-up cigarette. All in black I asked if it was not a touch warm for such clothes. "Only if you are a coward" was her reply. I laughed. She was interesting from the start. An independent thinker, she told me, no longer swayed by peer pressure. She did have money as a priority, but only for practical purposes. She had finished an IT course as she enjoyed programming, but had a dreadful memory so was not sure she would continue. In answer to my inevitable question, she would love to be a dog groomer. I had no idea what to say in reply. I could only think of Crufts pedigree dogs. She made a point of telling me that the chat was interesting, however, when we disembarked.

Later, in Bute Park, I sat on a bench with **Anne** who was reading a book about 'walking the talk' of the Lord's prayer. She was a little older than me, and an enthusiastic and excited speaker. We talked about many things, randomly jumping from one to another. She was entirely at ease that I declared myself to be atheist.

We even had an arena of common ground for she believed for sure that everything is connected. That the universe is one giant web. She had even read a Christian book that had *quantum* in the title. And we talked on the *impermanence* of things in part because she had recently started decluttering her house. Each trip to the tip or charity shop lightened her mind as well as her house. She agreed with me when I suggested it might be quite cathartic.

Her parting words were to hope that the Lord would give me a great life. It is hard not to endorse that. She also said that when asked, God declared that the meaning of life is *love*. And the way in which she connected with me showed that she walked *that* talk.

SEP 19 Victorin

One of my far neighbours, Brad has a French wife, **Victorin**, and baby girl. Today was the first time I spoke with her, a lady maybe more intriguing even than Brad. She was speaking in French to the baby. A trilingual baby, learning French, Welsh and English. At one point, **Victorin** mentioned her father in law. She pronounced the word 'law' just like Inspector Clouseau (Peter Sellars) in *The Pink Panther* films when he said that he was an *inspector of the law*. It was hard to suppress laughter!

SEP 21 Abergavenny food festival

Every September, Abergavenny hosts a large food festival. Not all years is it blessed with the blue sky and 24C heat that we gloried in today. So I emboldened myself for a near two hour bus journey and resumed my scenery gazing hobby.

It was in Cwmbran, I believe, that a lady a little older than I boarded and sat next to me. She was an easy talker and good listener, and we embarked on a thirty minute chat. Near the end of our chat, I declared that I was really enjoying talking but as an introvert was equally getting tired. It was a sign of her ease with me that I could say that. She also said the same, and we were, briefly as if one person. Quite a comforting feeling.

It transpires that **Mair De-Gare Pitt**, for that is her unusual name, is a published writer. Mostly poetry. She teaches also, and when seeking an artist to illustrate a recent book discovered that one of her students was more than capable for the task. Surprisingly, some of her former oil paintings matched some of the poems implausibly well. I necessarily mentioned that I was also a writer and that I was writing this book. I regaled the most recent story involving **Boyd Clack** only to discover that she knows him as he had attended one of her poetry sessions. Quite the small, connected world it seems.

After we agreed to stop talking, she read a book, so I also gave her one of my books to take away. I listened to music on headphones. After parting at our destination, I soon found a lady in ancient clothing to photograph. I captured her and realised that the lady she was talking with was in fact **Mair.**

Alas, the food festival was a heavily commercialised affair, costing rather a lot more than I was prepared to pay to enter the main areas. Fortunately, there were other food stalls scattered around, the sun was shining, the sky was a deep blue, and there were seemingly a million people energising this most delightful of Welsh towns.

Eventually, I had to eat and felt drawn to the exact same meal as I ate on my only previous visit here, at a wonderfully quirky department store called *Nicholls*. The most delicious and delightfully presented mini-lasagne with salad and garlic bread. Just enough on a hot day. I sat with an Irish family – two girls and father, with mother away on a circus event. And the father engaged me in dialogue the whole time I sat there.

Here you can see the restaurant at the rear of the shop with its high atrium flooding light in a cascade downward. I sat right in the corner most illuminated. My companion was a business marketing and campaigning man. He stressed that he operated on the ethical side of this game, promoting fairly. His children were extraordinarily well behaved, and clearly, he was a good father to them from what I could see. *Tough love* he described his approach – clear and consistent boundaries that regularly got contested of course, but always love at root.

I set off on a walk about among the madding crowds afterwards, and eventually found myself approaching a man with a fine mane of hair. I felt compelled to say hello. Sometimes I get nervous thinking about doing this. So I tend to jump straight in before my brain freezes. Only moments after speaking I impulsively asked if he was a bass guitarist. I was not far wrong as he sings in a band called *Damn Craters* based in Nottingham.

His daughter seemed upset and tired but was, he said, just shy. So I should have swiftly set out on my way. But I got embroiled in talking about influences to his band. And discovered Black Sabbath to be key catalyst for their style (have a listen and that is quite clear). I had bought the first four Sabbath albums with a friend when younger.

I discovered that Abergavenny has a delightful park, and headed for it mid afternoon. I found myself sat on a bench chatting with a very friendly mother of three children, one of whom was autistic. She was saying to me how she likes to avoid labelling him, but has a friend with an autistic boy that does so and it feels to the lady sat with me that this is stymying that boy's development.

She comes to the park most days since they live so close. She had reached the delightful point where she could safely let her boys wander quite far, although she did lose track of conversation a number of times as she lost sight of one or other of the boys. Some pictures of the park are shown on the next page.

There was a large queue for the bus back to Cardiff, so I nearly found myself standing. A lady made space on the luggage rack for me to sit next to her. **Mair** was stood in front of me also. An 83 year old Chinese man made us all laugh with one quip he made and the most enormous and natural smile so beguiling to follow. Later he could be seen sat with his similarly aged wife contentedly in the land of nod, with heads bowed forward as if joined in prayer together.

A couple to my left and a self-conscious lady to the left of **Mair** made a great base for conversation. The 'make-do' effort of coping with an overcrowded bus created a kind of war-time united community. Barriers of status melted away.

After some forty minutes or so, I was blessed with a seat and soon a lady of mixed Indian and African blood sat next to me. And chatted me to near exhaustion again. But a kind of content, benign state rather than a frazzled one. Of the many things we talked about, the African notion of frying sweet potato with sugar on it sounded appealing. The day was so long and tiring it felt like I was once again in full time work.

The tiredness enveloping me was also one of contentment.

Abergavenny

Psychology student

After gym work, I felt unusually energised and clear headed, so the notion of simply reading in the coffee shop was less attractive than normal. I wanted to talk, and I was particularly happy that the lady on the next table was willing to oblige. Studying her A levels, she was energised, curious minded and a great listener. That was probably vital as I was in full-on *pressure-of-speech* mode.

Her name was **Seren**, and she is studying Biology, Maths (I believe that she said) and Psychology. Her name means *star* in Welsh, and she was happy to talk about psychology as she hoped to study the subject at University. She was a delight to chat with.

One matter that we talked of was her desire to chat with strangers – precisely what she was doing with me. It was something she was keen to do but had not yet been so good at, she felt. I promoted the idea to her, but with a caveat of caution because she was attractive and young.

After a while, I asked her if my torrent of words was tiring her. She genuinely said that it was not, but she agreed with me on my comparison of introversion with extroversion. I related to her my current feeling that the interesting things that can arise in conversation can be the things that tire out the introverted type. What lures us in eventually can then push us away. Extroverts, by comparison, have such a high threshold for averting boredom that they rarely get overwhelmed by conversation.

I decided, as I thought on the fly in our conversation, that introverts must therefore be on the autistic spectrum – that the details in conversation that wash over extroverts can overwhelm introverts. Likewise, those 'suffering' with ADHD may also be on the spectrum, where details around can distract them from what they should be paying attention to. I mentioned *antaphasia* to her and she swiftly announced that only recently she had read an article about it – that the term was only created a few years ago. I gave **Seren** a copy of one of my books.

Later in the day, I received an email from **Nancy**. I had been able to access her web site at last. She said she had enjoyed my book and sent me a pdf of a book she has written, illustrated by **Paul**. *The Feeding Machine* is clearly a book written in a very unusual style. A novel, it seems, but with references to social development articles and concepts. It really makes me want to talk again with her. I offer quotes and an illustration from that book on the next page.

"I work with computers," I ruminated, cryptic machines that have become small enough to slip inside one's pocket. Housed in an impenetrable shell of plastic, these ubiquitous things can absorb one into a revolutionary 'other' world.

Using his concept of 'picnolepsy', Virilio suggests that modern perception has transformed our relationship with duration and de-synchronisation of time through cinematic technologies and spatial narratives of disappearance, affecting our sense of reality and blurring what is real and what is of human fabrication.

Chanel and Rickie

A blustery, autumnal day, with fast rushing clouds and injections of rain at random times. Time to try to find a book on the subject of architectural detail that caught my interest recently – fascinated again by all the little carvings and extravagances around windows and at the tops of buildings. Cardiff is blessed with many such 'artworks' as it were. The lady on the bus next to me was absorbed in her mobile phone – at least until the driver announcement of a detour when I grabbed her attention.

Poor lady – she was now trapped in a chat with me! But seriously, it was not quite that bad. She was animated of nature with a very expressive smile, and seemed entirely happy to chat. I asked if she thought that it was my age that saw me prefer to look at the scenery go by rather than engage in electronic diversions. She said that the buildings were boring – but that she did indeed love looking at sunlight greenery go past. This was a nice surprise – revealing how terribly easy it is to pigeon-hole the young.

She is a fitness instructor, hailing from the valleys with a strong accent. A lilting, rhythmic accent. A while back she went to a sports open day of sorts and discovered that she is a very good 200m runner. Most strange! This discovery solicited a move away from her first degree in film into fitness work. And now she was combining both of these themes – with clear excitement in her voice – with a masters degree in *sports film*. How curiously arbitrary events in our life can be that steer us.

She admitted to being a constant thinker as well as a clearly flexible, adaptive creature. Most friendly and engaging to talk with – implausibly good entertainment on a humble bus journey. Her name was **Chanel**, just like the perfume.

On the bus home from town, I decided the crowd of youngsters at the back were a bit too noisy and I took a stop earlier than normal. By doing so, I bumped into **Rickie**, a very warm *Scope* charity worker I had bumped into a couple of days ago. I had given him a copy of "Improve your life" and he was saying now that he was already on chapter three and loving it. That of course is a nice thing to hear. To help someone with emotional problems.

His girlfriend also wants to read the book.

Saturday morning after a magnificent night of sleep, I was fired up for a mix of reading and chatting, the former for sure, the latter if fortunate. Coffee #1 tends to be pretty busy on Saturdays so I was denied a comfy chair window seat, instead quite happy to sit on a wooden chair at a table upstairs in the window, the sun blasting in sweet heat in-between heavy downpours. I had no less than four books to read after the library trip yesterday. One on the current state of journalism (*Breaking News*), another on the art of designing *logos*, and finally a splendid Taschen book on the subject of *illustration* with a vast diversity of styles from an array of artists. I had been very narrow with my reading of late and this was fun.

Two boys appeared, followed by their mother, choosing to sit in the comfy chairs near to me. She was a pleasure to chat with, and such a good listener that I feared I had bombarded her. I am trying to fine tune my verbosity, to rein it in as appropriate, but she declared herself most happy with the chat. One of her boys was how my brother **Ian** looked when young, and was equally quiet, waiting to say something profound rather than filling in the chat gaps. Again, just like my brother. His younger brother was slouched in his chair, flippant to his mother, but when I asked him what he thought of Boris Johnson as a person, he declared that he could not say as he only saw him as a politician. I had to admire this sharpness of understanding.

They left and were soon replaced by a very friendly young man. How often, you see me say, that people I meet are friendly. The truth is that most people are indeed friendly when you greet them with genuine warmth. His name was **Duncan** and he was no longer a student but instead applying his chemistry degree in research on energy efficient devices. I honour his preference that I do not mention the company or details of his work. Suffice to say is that they were making great progress on two fronts in a time when energy efficiency is becoming ever more vital.

A friend of his appeared after a while, climbing into a sprawling posture, draped across the other comfy chair, and it was like watching an A grade film star bursting with presence. An extremely handsome man with an enchanting, beaming smile above a small black beard. His face was very precisely structured. I asked **Duncan** what his friend did for a living as I felt sure he should be an actor in films. He said that I was not far wrong as he is a cameraman. And a singer in a band as well as an occasional drummer. The world of expression was, it seemed, very much his oyster. I stayed a while in chat with them as they both seemed comfortable that I did. One of the habits I have is to try to fine tune my perception my impact on others. To sense the fine clues that dialogue is on track or losing its sheen.

Meanwhile, **Ed** had arrived to sit on my other side. I remarked that he looked most particularly healthy – simply because he did. He too had noticed a change in his appearance in the last few days and had tried to work out why that might be the case. He presumed that an addition of omega 3 fatty acids and another such change might have been the cause. His girlfriend arrived with a matching smile, but when I talked to the two of them I felt she was a bit wary of me so I drew back into my books.

A couple of hours equally exciting and tiring. I left feeling vitalised, with some recovery of energy after twenty minutes of post-chat reading. Such mornings tend to permit time all alone for the remainder of the day with no feel of being lonely. A kind of stockpile of connection with others. A recharging of sociability.

SEP 29   At the Lidl checkout

After shopping at my local Lidl supermarket, a lady near me was in limbo, with just one item, it seemed. I said she was welcome to go in front of me. She declined as she said that she did not like the lady on the checkout. I risked it, but the checkout woman did look frumpy and ready to snap at anyone who did not 'toe the line' on checkout 'rules'. Except that she was none of these things. Instead, she was particularly warm and friendly when I got to the checkout. She was so nice that I had to reflect that I could not remember the last I was served who was so radiantly happy a person to greet me as a customer.

I wonder what the avoidant lady had done to miss this?

Later in the day, the three children of one of the Iraqi families in my road were keen to chat when we met as they were walking to their home. They are particularly polite and engaging, so I have a lot of time for them. The youngest, about four, is most sweet, with a creative imagination. He asked if I do *sciency* things. I said I read about psychology so he asked me what that was about. So divine to engage with children like this. Later still, the four boys of the other Iraqi family accosted me with smiles and inquiries. Do I play tennis every day? How am I?

All quite in contrast to an all too common Welsh/British 'reserve' which we cling to as a defining part of our 'culture'. We really should challenge this aloofness.

Three chats in succession

A grey day, with no prospects of sun, alas. But it is not so much a problem when my schedule is gym work followed by reading and chatting in a coffee shop. The same routine I have followed countless times, but the people I met today diminished that sense of sameness to nearly nothing. It was like being a rogue invitee to an event held for extraordinarily nice people.

I sat upstairs with my back to the window so that my reading was illuminated by the light of day, even though not a sunny one. I turned around briefly to say hello to the lady who was reading "Wuthering Heights" at her table. My head craned to do so, and stayed there rather longer than a moment. Maybe half an hour? How can I say that I met another smiling lady without making it seem that I am somehow elaborating? She beamed at me as if I was special. And then she proceeded to outdo me with her fast flowing thought train. But all coherent and appropriate to the things we discussed, such as her English Literature degree and soon to be resumed Masters degree in the same subject. She writes children's stories, she thinks and thinks and thinks, and also therefore proclaimed that she thinks too much. Her name was **Sophie** and I was spell-bound. Such an exquisitely fascinating creature. So energised and so thrilled about being alive – about embracing what life threw at her, including challenging her University on its declared equal rights policy, yet to be denied the necessary child minding support from them to be able to work on her Masters. A hyperactive five year old is too demanding and distracting to allow her to focus on her work.

She was necessarily thrilled when I gave her a couple of my books to read. I wanted to know her reaction to my short novel, and also to encourage her to retry meditation. She is weaning herself away from her phone, and very much would like to calm her ceaselessly active mind. She thanked me for addressing another matter – I had asked to read her short stories, and so she now had some motivation for putting them online, maybe coupling them with the art work others had volunteered to her. She had delayed on this idea as procrastination, she revealed, was a weakness of hers. I suggested maybe a consequence of too much time thinking and too little doing. But I made a point that thinking deeply itself was intrinsically good, even if sometimes needing some constraining or tempering.

This was a thrilling but exhausting chat, not least because I had to concentrate hard to listen carefully to her long, but fascinating thought streams. Maybe that tiredness was the cause of a rare symptom at one point where I suddenly felt a kind of detachment. A feeling that my mind might want to escape the dialogue and say something sarcastic. This is pretty unsettling stuff. But I did not feel too bad about myself that this matter was intruding, not least because I did not choose this and it was out of context. So I did not buy into this intrusion and let it fade. It was a tiny existential crisis, if that makes sense.

Not long after she left, **Delon** arrived. A smart, slim, handsome, interesting looking fellow. Like **Sophie**, I would guess that he was in his twenties (everyone under fifty looks young to me). A computer programmer, and clearly a well informed and articulate man, his name is French apparently, the emphasis being placed on the second syllable. Yet he is South African. My ADHD blurted out the belief that these are friendly people. He said that this is said often but he felt that it was generally true of most countries. And that some of the divisions that apartheid created are unfortunately bubbling up again.

Delon also had a disarming smile, albeit a gentle one. Less dominant than many big-smilers I meet. But I struggled to match his intellect. When we talked about psychiatric drugs, in particular those for depression called Serotonin Re-Uptake Enhancers, he subsequently referred to them as SSRIs, the medical abbreviation that I had seen in the book on the subject. The son of a wealthy man he knew was given pre-release *prozac* tablets, presumably to help with depression. **Delon** described some strange behaviours that resulted from this, and how in general anti-depressants tend to fade in effect over time, but the takers oddly continue to extol their efficacy or virtues. It would be nice to talk to him again, especially when not so tired as I now was.

So why did I then proceed to talk with an 'A' level student who now sat in the window seat? I have no idea. Maybe I was on a roll.

I was now blessed with a third enchanting person. Her name was **Kacie**, and she was an introvert who was originally shy but now loved to talk to strangers. The animated smile adorning her face – one that showed no sign of hiding any feelings or thoughts – was that of a seasoned talker. A practiced engager. Yet she was probably only seventeen years old.

It is worth asking, I feel, if you see such chats as *just* chats – simply a form of retirement fun? Since I often write about such chats here, and this book may yet get published and sell copies, then is it not work also?

OCT 1 — Chatting with Declan again

Last night I came down with symptoms of a head cold. As is my habit, I fed my body to fight that invasion. Lots of overeating. But the symptoms remained, albeit pretty low-key, this morning. However, I found myself strangely in a happier frame of mind than normal. Very few people seem to notice that in the early stages of a cold, the mind shuts down its highly intrusive, constant chatter habit. I felt distinctly calmer than normal. A mellow contentment that only tends to get disrupted when the symptoms ramp up and become tediously intrusive.

So it was nice to read a little before another chat with **Declan**. We spoke calmly, as his natural way, about the process of writing lyrics. For him, they precede melody, but only for a short while. After early word ideas have been created, a melody to fit them creates the platform for repeated iterations of word and sound. He said that he would still like to be able to find a creative mind-state more readily, and we both agreed that meditation would help free up his subconscious to have a greater voice. But, as seems common, he found meditation on the breath to be awkward and ineffective. After giving him some alternative ideas, I asked that he feed back to me how he gets on.

OCT 3 — Ladies from Iran

With a sniffling mild cold, I survived the gym and avoided feeling sorry for myself. There are two ladies that I occasionally see in Coffee #1 who sit to chat in animated style, always proffering me smiles when I pass by. One arrived early today and I went to talk with her. Most people who smile at others in coffee shops do so in a kind of reflex, automatic manner. The smile that **Layla** offered lit up her whole face, and was most certainly genuinely heartfelt. I mentioned how my neighbouring Iraqi family smile also. And that they had offered me a typical Iraqi meal. **Layla** upped the stakes! She invited me to come to her house where she would cook me a typical Iranian meal, so that I can declare which cuisine I like most. How generous to someone she barely knows.

Her friend arrived and matched **Layla**'s smile. My own smile in return felt most inadequate!

I received an email from **Åsa**, the lady in the photograph on the next page that I frequently see working in Coffee #1. She is most accommodating of my interrupts to her typing. And a delight to talk with, in part because her work revolves around people. She included this in her email :

> *I am encountering much synchronicity in my current state of openness, having allowed curiosity space in my life. It was good to read about your travels and encounters and also to find out a little bit about what drives you to talk to strangers. I have always found it fascinating to watch you connect with people.*

Clearly, a key to connecting well with strangers is the curiosity she refers to. It draws you into the world of others. It is not so much nosiness, which is generally a route to gossip, but more intrigue, to explore an interest in how others live their lives. To engage in diversity.

A different kind of interaction

Last night was chillingly hard to handle. Starting at midnight, and lasting around about four hours, I suffered an elevated heart rate, body spasms, extreme agitation and so on. Another panic attack – but by far the longest so far in my life.

Most surprisingly, the day that followed has been wonderful so far. Sure, I am hanging-tired, but in an upbeat, resilient mood. Maybe a sense of happiness in the resilience I demonstrated for surviving last night and also learning from the doctor that it was very much unlikely to be a genuine heart problem. Having been very reluctant to endure my normal early morning gym session, especially as the elevated heart rate on the cycle machine can trigger anxiety, I nevertheless decided to go anyway just before lunch.

Which meant a different crowd of people. After cycling to get my heart rate up to 140 b.p.m. with no ill-effects, I sat on the rowing machine. A man near me was balancing on one leg, so I asked him if he had tried doing this with his eyes shut. If he could last fifteen seconds, I said, that he would be doing well. And I discovered this man to be how I must be with others – very keen to sustain a chat, very open and embracing. It was odd to be on the receiving end of someone who was very keen to connect to others. But I was so tired, it felt odd that someone would be keen to talk with me.

Somehow or other, talk of physicality triggered **Chris Lewis** to talk about the junior football club **Ty Celyn** that he is secretary for. He encouraged me to join in and help if I was interested. I told him about the recreation field community football games I have played in, and he said that there were grants if I wanted to start a veterans team. Clearly, **Chris** was a very giving person. He asked if I had attended the *Homeless World Cup*. Of all the fifty teams that played in it, can you believe that Chris coached the *Norwegian Ladies Team*, and therefore knew **Rona** very well?

What chance is there if a connection like this?

He suggested that I go to the next world cup in Finland. It does, strange to say, sound quite enticing. To have a social focal point in a foreign land organised in advance.

There was absolutely nothing that I could perceive that might have made me choose this man to talk to in the hope of finding some synchronicity. And I really was so dull in the head that the thought of this book was far from my mind.

Sunday morning chats

My throat was sore, but the words flowed. At least for a while. A tall, vibrant looking lady I do not recall seeing before came upstairs in Coffee #1, with book in hand. I asked about it, and she came over to my table to show me. A book about a musician, so I asked her if she was a singer. I got it wrong again – precisely the wrong way round – as she was a bass guitarist, from Slovenia. We chatted about how bass supplies more of the foundation and rhythm of songs than most people are aware. She works in PR and adopts the same, subtle approach to that work as with her guitar.

After a while, a family sat near me, starting first with the father, a most friendly and chatty fellow. An engineer but also a creative type. As was his ten year old daughter who loves doing creative drawing. When all faced and chatted with me, broad and natural smiles beaming at me, I again felt a little overwhelmed and inadequate. A certain self-doubt can arise from time to time. But it tends to fade. Suffice to say, they were a delight to meet, agreeing with me that they broke the mould of British reserve. And that included the girl, more comfortable engaging in direct eye-contact with a stranger than most her age would typically be.

An 'awkward' day

Fortunately, days like this tend to be pretty rare. It was the day to catch the bus to my dentist in St Melons for my six-monthly dental checkup. Shortly into the outward bound journey, an elderly man shuffled onto the bus, aided by two walking sticks. I made space for him to sit next to me as I was in one of the disabled seats. Unusually, he started talking to me before I greeted him. But I sensed from the start a monologue type talking style. But I could not be sure, so I asked him about his condition, for he also wore special 'gloves' on his hands.

He explained that he had *Coeliac's* disease, where the immune system attacks the body. Without his special hand-wear, his hands would tighten into fists. I asked if he had knee or hip problems, but he said that it was actually a whole body problem. The poor man.

But he was speeding up his chat and starting to feel liberated into an unleashing of complaints about his motorised vehicle and other such matters. I was tensing up because this was no conversation, but an unloading. Much as I felt sympathy for his plight, I kind of knew he would not understand that I needed to stop chatting so as to ease my tensing head. Otherwise, it would create a bigger headache than the one I now had. So I asked (told him?) if I could put my headphones on.

I did not feel guilty but relieved. But plagued now by a small, residual headache that I did not have ten minutes earlier.

No problems at the dentist, fortunately. Walking along the aisle of the bus on the way home a familiar face spotted me and insisted I sit with her. A very friendly, earnest, authentic lady from five or so years back. But, alas, a very loud, intense and demanding type, largely indifferent to or unaware of her impact on others. I told her straight away that I could sit but would listen to music because of my headache. She was fine, but she forced kisses on each cheek, and unleashed a verbal bombardment. Sometimes, it hurts my ears when someone sat so close is this loud and intense. But it is very hard to be annoyed at her, and in a sense I was not, because she is a good person. A very giving person. But I had to don headphones again.

Except that a looooooong phone call she now embarked on was uncomfortably loud even with ear protection.

The effect of this lady in the past was diluted in a group of five to ten that used to meet in the garden of Sereno Restaurant in Albany Road. There was something very special about this rag-bag of eccentric and off-beat characters. That these oft-marginalised types of people can actually be more accommodating of people with difficult lives than those blessed with an 'ordinary' existence. There were no less than five of this varying group of characters that had been diagnosed with *bipolar disorder*. All were medicated I believe – at least all seemed particularly calm of nature to the point that it would have been hard to believe they were not neurotypical. Sadly, one or two of the people who attached to this near-daily gathering were destructive of the ethos, as well as being chronic alcoholics. Their influence became too caustic, so I stopped meeting there. The place has long since closed.

I left the bus early to escape my feeling of entrapment/sensory-overload and walked to Waterloo Tea shop, on the way home. A window seat beckoned, but as I entered, the lady in the queue was about to sit there. She was absolutely fine about conceding the seat to me.

But this was a third awkwardness, so I later went over to where she sat so that I could give her a copy of one of my books. I asked if she read. She did not – her ONC Engineering studies had put her off reading for life. But she saw the book in my hand and I talked about it. She was keen to read. Quite energetically so. A while later, she came over to my seat and asked if I would not mind signing the book. I duly obliged.

A little younger than I, she came across as a very warm person. If my head was not straining so much from the days events (even reading was a bit tricky), then I might well have talked further with her. But her return for signature lifted my spirits a little even though I tried to learn from the bus incidents rather than allow them to define how I should feel.

OCT 9 On subsequent meetings

Talia made some very good points to me for this book a few days ago. Not least, she felt that I should describe how subsequent meetings with strangers I meet pan out, and to ask them, as tactfully as possible, how they found me when I initially started talking with them.

It just so happens that I have seen **Delon** most days since we first chatted, so I can answer the first question, even if anecdotally for just one person. I spoke with him again today in **Coffee #1** so I mentioned the second question to him and asked him to ponder his response (I did not get a reply before his subsequent emigration).

He is a charming young man, I presume in his twenties, who is a clear and lucid thinker, as well as being curious- and nimble-minded. So he has been an ongoing delight to talk with. We kind of energise each other, and catalyse more conversation by piquing the curiosity of the other. Today, for example, we talked about the actual nature of *empathy* as opposed to the shallow, simplistic view most have. So now I have a book recommendation to follow – *Against Empathy*.

When I saw him for this second time, the feeling is of course very different from the first time, where spontaneity is more possible. There can be a negative feeling of social obligation in subsequent meetings that can lead to avoidance if the first meeting was tricky. But I try to greet with a light, jovial attitude, hoping that this allows for as brief or sustained a chat as the other person chooses or wants at this moment. It is always the case with **Delon** that he is accommodating, always stopping laptop work to chat. And I often talk about his work – remote programming – and how he can struggle to stay focussed so far from the business base.

I guess that sustaining a friendship that was initiated by accident when two strangers meet is down to the simple reality of sufficient shared interests. With **Delon**, I have met a gem of a person with much common ground. Today I asked if he would like to read one of the books I have written. I presented four, and he asked to take all of them away in order to make a better choice. When he saw that I had written fiction, he said that he too was a novel writer, but that he rarely completed ideas. We discussed this, and it seems that this is not a problem of procrastination or discipline, but that it was more a path he must follow – to keep pursuing ideas and keep writing, and eventually a book will be completed. To pressurise a creative process felt intrinsically wrong to him.

OCT 10 — Louise and Pascal

One of the ladies I greeted at the gym I attend is a swarthy, Amazon-type, raven-haired beauty. Today was the first time I properly chatted with her. We were sat on adjacent rowing machines, paused ready to sweat carbohydrates and extend sinews. When I replied to her question of how I was feeling today with a brief description of my series of panic attacks, she too declared she suffered with these. Her name is **Louise** and she is also a worrier, easily affected by others – in effect she cares too much. That someone who ostensibly looked so relaxed could equally suffer as I do was a revelation. It made me wonder how many others we see as robustly healthy have hidden problems we could not guess at.

To Waitrose after lunch and a chat with a stranger. Except that he was not. It dawned on him after ten minutes that we had chatted before. **Pascal** is a warm, coherent, friendly man in his thirties or forties. A market researcher by trade, so we ended up talking about supermarkets with bread making facilities operating the ovens all day so that the smell could keep enticing customers in through the door. And to position these bakeries at the rear of the shop to maximise the chance they would buy other produce on the way to the source of the smell.

I made the point that marketing tends to operate with deception and customer manipulation at its core. He agreed, and it was odd that this should be the nature of his job as he also worked to teach Christianity to Chinese immigrants. Not sure how we got onto that theme, but he was in full flow now, and I was a silent listener. For once. But it was not hard as he was a clear narrator. It puzzled him not so much that the Chinese work ethic should make adjustment to British life a slow process, but it was how terribly *narrow* their lives were made by that work ethic that in turn made progress so slow.

The very notion of taking time to worship – to respect life and the planet that supports it – was just missing from their days in China. Work, work, work was pretty much all they knew. There was very little time to smile, to socialise, to laugh, to enjoy hobbies. It was like they were now thawing out, and in the process the starkness of their decades of ardour painfully dawning upon them.

Pascal was delighted to chat with me . His face was so alive with the excitement of sharing parts of his life. This is pretty special, so I felt honoured in a sense that the simple act of listening should solicit so warm a response.

OCT 11 Chatting with Jason again

Not sure if I have mentioned **Jason** before. I met him in Coffee #1 in Wellfield Road a few months ago. He sat with me today. Much like **Delon**, a man in his twenties or thirties, and engaging and easy to talk with. When I discovered that the work he most likes to do is film set development, I shared with him some potentially influential films. And we discovered a deeply felt mutual love of 2001 *A space Odyssey* and the Studio Ghibli film *Ponyo*. We sit there enthusing in unison about the brilliance behind these creations. Yet not so long ago, this man was a stranger to me.

I made a mental note to recover from a friend a boxed set of *Pressberger and Powell* films from the 1950's that I would guess **Jason** would like to watch, including my two favourites *A matter of life and death* and *Black Narcissus*.

OCT 12 Morgan

Yet another trip to Waterloo Tea shop, but absent the sun. I miss its warming, calming influence. A young man seated nearby was surprisingly happy to chat. He is a director of *motor racing* videos in a small business, posting their output on Youtube via their company *Alpha Live* channel, with 200+ videos and 8,000+ subscribers at the time of writing. Modern life is moving ever faster away from traditional jobs and traditional companies. Startups abound.

His name was **Morgan Jones** and he was a little nervous in chat, but energetic and enthusiastic once he got going. I discovered from him that this tea shop does hot water teapot top-ups. We talked about production and films but also his declared trouble sticking intensely with one thing. I offered him my view that a problem that would seem hard to overcome is often precisely the type that would likely give the highest rewards for overcoming. Not sure I convinced him, but I like to think so.

OCT 13 Such a wonderful young man to chat with on the bus

The morning was blighted by a headache along with face muscles tightened into a knot. No idea after good sleep why I should awaken to this very uncomfortable state. So I tend to ignore it. But today it was making me feel very *physically* depressed, about to burst into tears at any moment. As if I had heard very sad news – the pulled down face muscles were generating a physical feeling of sadness, where smiling was a struggle. Yet the strangest thing is that my *mood* was upbeat. I was literally physically sad and emotionally happy at the same time. Well, nearly – I could flip focus between the two. This is kind of insane, but I am not insane.

I hope I do not allow too many of my maladies to intrude on the narrative. They are included to give a more rounded context to my meetings with others. First, to show that they do not always have to be impediments to conversation, to engagement with others. Second, that behind the scenes most people we assume are ostensibly healthy have flaws and problems – we humans tend to hide a great deal. Especially the British. Third, that instead of succumbing to problems, withdrawing into our plight, and thereby potentially exacerbating it, we can extend beyond ourselves and energise via distraction.

At the bus stop on the way home, while I was still feeling the powerful pull of depression, a ludicrously slim young man arrived and stood near me. I asked him if he ate a lot as surprisingly many people with his physique do, and get away with it, staying slim. But he said he did not eat much, and then proceeded to tell me that he slept a lot. His favourite was a twenty hour sleep. How crazy, yet this man was clearly coherent and sane. And so supremely happy to talk with me. We chatted as if long term friends, my talk upbeat and happy, in complete contrast to my physical condition.

We continued conversation sat side by side on the bus. He is doing his 'A' levels with a view to studying Civil Engineering at Cardiff University. A passion of his, having watched and helped his father's Civil Engineering business from the tender age of three.

I wish I could capture the energy and enthusiasm of this man, utterly at ease talking to a balding, middle aged man with a plaster on his head (on the outbound bus I gouged the top of my head on the wing mirror and yielded an impressive flow of blood – passengers gave me tissues and a sticking plaster!) His parents are both Italian, and one grandparent Arabic. His name, I believe, was **Emilo**, but I might have missed an 'L' out. His friends call him *mile-oh*. He works at the John Lewis department store, and necessarily learns a great deal about human nature and dialogue, clearly relishing his contacts with others. One time recently, he said, he saw a thirteen year old bump into a seventy-five year old, too engrossed on his phone to see him. A heated argument ensued. This intrigued **Emilo** who rarely uses his mobile phone.

He says that many young people who come into the shop struggle immensely to string complete sentences together, and rarely make eye contact. He is as alarmed at this status of disconnect as I am. My stop arrived too soon, and I had not given him a book as token of the encounter. So I think I will remedy this by visiting the store where he works later this week. I feel deeply compelled to retain a connection with a man of such vitality, with conversation skills that far outstrip most adults. How did he learn such eloquent and articulate speaking and listening skills by the late teens? A truly remarkable young man. (I did later visit the shop but it is vast and all departments are independently run. So there was no central register of employee names).

Later in the day at Waterloo tea shop (I really must seek out new venues ...) I encountered a very friendly mother and her grown-up daughter. The former, **Sue**, is a retired specialist dyslexia teacher, her daughter **Amy** works in University marketing. I mention this couple as further examples of how implausibly friendly some people can be. The sheer accepting manner in which these ladies allowed me to talk to them was as if I was about to deliver them a winners cheque in a lottery. Except it was better than that as it was not predicated on any acquisition. **Sue** took a couple of my books, to read and pass on.

OCT 15 Lucid dreaming

I realised this morning that **Delon** is quite remarkably bright and articulate. But these faculties are coupled with, and enhanced by, an inquisitive, insightful mind, which propels my own mind to think more clearly than normal, and to be more coherent in my speech. He was ahead of me in the coffee shop queue, clearly day-dreaming. So I asked him out of curiosity where that was taking him. And this lead to a chat about dreams, and how my sister Carol not only remembers most dreams, but most are *lucid*. This is where you become aware you are dreaming. A kind of emergent consciousness when ostensibly asleep! It is something that has intrigued me immensely, and now I discover that this was the case for **Delon** also. As a youngster, he tried to train his mind to give greater chance of lucid dreaming. The curious mind is nothing without action driven by that curiosity. He was able to achieve partial success in his goal.

I explained to him that one of the things I love to do when lucid whilst asleep is to see how realistic the dream is. To explore how well reality is rendered. And the astounding conclusion that I came to is that dream rendering is implausibly realistic. This truly, deeply baffles me. For me, such strangeness is like a red rag to a bull. I was once in a shop in a dream. I stopped and moved my head around to see if the scene tracked that movement. It did. Flawlessly as far as I could ascertain. Another time, I stood atop a ridge with a tree lined valley spread out below me. Panning again saw no loss of realism. Yet this was a place I do not ever recall going to. I walked close to a tree and the bark was vivid and realistic.

Most mysterious was on a bus on a rainy day in a dream. I observed the refraction of light through the water droplets on the window as the scenery sped past. I simply do not believe that my brain can render this detail in real time. Compare with cinema animations that use CGI. Each second of film comprises 24 or 25 frames – a picture rendered in each. The rendering of just one picture takes powerful computers the best part of a day, thousands of times slower than projection speed. So where does my brain source what I see? It cannot store memories as 'movies' because it does not know how I will move my head around them in the dream. They also do not look like two dimensional memories rendered to look three dimensional.

Delon and I wondered if we were accessing scenes outside of ourselves. It seems unfeasible, but how else to explain what lucid dreaming reveals to me? The martial art he practices describes our consciousness in two parts – the body, ego-bound aspect, and the etherial, outward part. Maybe lucid dreaming is a window to the latter? The logical, scientific parts of my brain reject this. But the aesthetic, expansive parts do not.

Later in the day, as is my new habit, I went for a walk in one of Cardiff's many parks. It is, apparently, the greenest city in the UK, and has the top two parks for tree diversity (public arboretums). At one point, the late afternoon sun shone a narrow band of light into the otherwise darkening park. It wonderfully illuminated a single, grand tree. What a splendid sight to behold!

I was not alone in that feeling, for a lady, presumably in her twenties, stood nearby mesmerised by the same vision. I shared my feelings of the scene before us and asked from a safe distance if she was a photographer. Whilst she was not, she was an aesthete, and an articulate, enthusiastic talker. She agreed that connecting to others, especially recreating communities was very important in a time where we as a nation seem hell bent on acting all too often in stark isolation.

We chatted a while at the same, now awkward distance. Her name was **Charlie** and she works in health risk assessment. She also reads voraciously (her word) in her spare time. She recommended a form of *stream of consciousness* writing in "A girl is a half-formed thing" by McBride. (The reviews were mixed when I later checked, but this may be no surprise when the writing style is so extreme).

I shook hands and set to depart but we were headed the same way so I walked with her for a few hundred yards until our routes diverged. She was easy to talk with, and I just regret that I did not have a book to give her to read. I had been lazy and not carried my backpack.

OCT 16 — Toby the woodworker

It is rare for me to encounter someone who is also a cabinet maker. I cannot remember when I last did, if ever. **Toby** was sat outside Waterloo Tea shop and I discovered this shared interest when I chatted with him. Conversation drifted to politics and dogs – his ludicrously large Alsatian at his side, scaring passers-by, but not meaning to. I mentioned this book and he suggested I listen to a Radio 4 programme on coincidences. I later did so (the programme aired on 12 March 2018) – and found it suitable intriguing.

The reporter on that programme, Rajesh Mirchandani, declared that he rarely encounters coincidences or synchronicities, but realised that he missed two key attributes that would have enabled these things better – observation of all around him, and the interest in speaking to strangers. My ADHD/Aspergers mind is frequently picking up on details so it is actually hard for me *not* to be aware of the myriad of things around myself. They often overwhelm me.

The programme, alas, sought to explain away these coincidences as statistically likely to happen. It did not seem to even entertain alternative explanations. A kind of scientific arrogance that permits itself denial as a matter of course.

OCT 18 — Toms Gamaliel Canevali

What an extraordinary encounter. But this was a stranger that I did not meet face to face. We shared a game of Go on the Internet. But more — much more than that — we shared a profound and deep chat about the philosophy and psychology of Go. **Toms** was supremely receptive to my talk of life skills pertaining to Go, where you get stronger when you release attachments to stones on the board. Where you see the big picture rather than allow small-fry matters to determine how you play.

He was very keen to chat and we will hopefully resume another day. Just before leaving, I discovered that he is studying a degree in Psychology in Argentina. And that he adores talking to strangers, adopting an attitude free from fear when he does so. A young man embracing what took me decades longer to encounter and engage with. The game and chat left me with a frisson of excitement. It really did.

OCT 21 — Get Britain Talking

A few days ago, the mothers of the two Iraqi families in my road that I have befriended were talking in front of one of their homes as I passed. They both gave me warm smiles. Then I realised that the head-wear of one had only a window for her eyes. And how delightful it was, therefore, to realise how much we smile with our eyes as well as with our mouth.

In the newspaper yesterday was a mental health initiative entitled *Get Britain Talking*. A key article had the title :

> *Open up: why connecting with others is the hidden ingredient to mental wellbeing*

And a subtitle :

> *Humans are innately social creatures, and the importance of making and keeping connections isn't news to us. But while reaching out isn't always easy, it is essential for your mental health – and that of those around you*

Hopefully, this will serve to convince you of the legitimacy of what I and many others do, of connecting with people wherever you go, in spite of impediments. It parallels work, where you have a group of fellow-workers that you connect with – *and who give you a sense of value and legitimacy* – because of the connections and shared purpose. I aim to create a shared purpose in those I meet by wanting to share life experiences with them.

It appears that one in four of UK families sit together using electronic devices and fail to talk with each other. This is astoundingly bad for their collective health. The article on the matter goes on to say :

> *Anyone who's had periods of feeling low or depressed will know it's easy to find yourself in a cycle where, because of those feelings, you avoid contact with other people and end up feeling even worse. It's at times like those that you need to try and remember the power of connecting with others – however difficult and daunting it may seem.*

OCT 23 Tiring chats

Some days when I enter Coffee #1 it happens that I barely get time to read a book. Of course, this is no hardship. Especially when talking with delightful people such as **Delon** and **Åsa** (who is so wonderfully excited about starting up a life-coaching business).

It was maybe half an hour before I could sit and read today, and by then, the conversation had tired me. So when a man came and sat at my table, in shorts on a cool day, I did not look up from my book to greet him. Besides, he just sat down without the normal custom of asking if OK to do so. And he looked the type who would be brusque in conversation.

After a while, however, I decided that I might be judging him falsely so talked with him. And he did indeed come across as warm and friendly, entirely at odds with the personality he projected in his movements. A reminder to me to be mindful of judgements.

As ever, such mindfulness is an ongoing matter – there is no destination or target to reach for.

OCT 24 Delon will be leaving

Just as I find *the* most interesting person to talk to *in my life*, I learn today that **Delon** is leaving Wales in a week. He is moving to Portugal, alas. This is devastating for me!

I was very curious why he felt driven to relocate. It transpires that he is joining a group of students of *Daoist Nei Gong* to study closer to their teacher, *Damo Mitchell*. The house he will live in is just ten minutes walk from Damo's house. He is necessarily excited, but equally disappointed that we will not be able to continue our rich, diverse and engaging conversations. I wait my whole life to find a counterpart of myself (even better – a smarter one) and this encounter is terminated barely after it starts.

I ordered *A comprehensive guide to Daoist Nei Gong* on **Delon**'s recommendation (along with the Amazon praises) in part because he said that it would help with my health, but also to share what might be contributing to **Delon**'s calm but curious and wise nature. It is written by Damo Mitchell.

Look inside ↓

A Comprehensive Guide to Daoist Nei Gong Paperback – Illustrated, 21 Aug 2018
by Damo Mitchell. Foreword by Paul Mitchell. (Author)
☆☆☆☆☆ ⌄ 18 ratings

› See all 2 formats and editions

Kindle Edition	Paperback
£16.24	£22.49 ✓prime
Read with Our Free App	3 Used from £21.58
	13 New from £20.58

Note: This item is eligible for **click and collect.** Details
Nei Gong is the practice leading to attainment of real internal skill and transformation, and the philosophical art of change that runs through all Daoist practice. This book provides a unprecedented insight into the entire Nei Gong process, expanding upon the foundations laid in the author's previous widely read book, Daoist Nei Gong, to provide a deeper and more comprehensive understanding of the practice. Going into unparalleled detail whilst remaining accessible, it explains the philosophy at the heart of Nei Gong practice, and the steps whereby transformation is achieved. A foundational knowledge of Chinese medicine will help the reader appreciate the explanation more deeply, but is not required for understanding. Essential reading for all serious practitioners of Qi Gong and the Daoist tradition, the book will also be an invaluable resource for anyone interested in Chinese medicine, martial arts or advanced meditation.

See all 2 images

As you can see, this a a book that I am keen to receive and read. We tentatively arranged to actually sit and have a coffee together before he departs. Hopefully **Talia** can join us.

Meanwhile, I feel compelled to mention two very different but equally brilliant books that I am reading.

The Ethical Capitalist by the owner of the *Richer Sounds* chain of music/video systems. For forty years, he has operated his business with a very sage, holistic set of ethical principles. He argues, with good reason, that doing so helps his business grow and remain profitable. Chasing profit is, he argues, like the tail wagging the dog. Not a good idea. I highly recommend you read this short book.

The other book is *Lifespan*, a learned and paradigm shifting book about the ageing process, with the central tenet that it is a *disease* not a feature of the human genome – a matter of digital (DNA) and analogue (epigenetic) information degeneration that can largely be mediated.

The author is an international expert on ageing, has thirty-five+ awards to his name, and appears to have well-supported research to back his notions. Whilst admitted as anecdotal, his father made two changes to his life in his mid seventies on the back of the book ideas and within a short time was literally climbing mountains. The author plays this down as anecdote, as he should, but it is a potential testament to the theories expounded.

OCT 25 Ted video on ageing

Whilst chatting with **Delon** this morning, he showed me a Ted video he had seen a few weeks ago that he was reminded of by my mentions of the *Lifespan* book. He now wants to take greater heed of the message of that video as it too was on the subject of ageing. And surprise, surprise, the talker was David Sinclair, author of *Lifespan*.

To town after lunch and a pot of tea in the John Lewis department store coffee shop, replete with aerial view of the street below. A couple and her mother asked if they could take the comfy chair in front of me. So it was a chance to chat. The mother was a fair bit older than me, but fully cognisant and energised. She was from Colchester but met a man in Manchester and went to Iraq to live in his country. She was alarmed at how that country was brutalised. We got to talking about politics and she declared that Jeremy Corbyn was not a good speaker. Clearly, this perception is in part a failure of the BBC to broadcast any of the many public speeches he has made, at venues where people have queued around the corner to enter. At one open air public speech, apparently ten thousand attended, with some climbing trees to get a good vantage point.

OCT 26 Oboe player

Saturday morning in Coffee #1 escaping relentless rain outside. When it rains in Wales, it admirably attempts to mimic Indian monsoons. **Delon** sat on a nearby table, and was joined by a series of friends, most older than himself. And being able to observe from afar, it occurred to me that he was not so similar from myself. He engages in an upbeat, positive, energised, non-judgemental fashion with all he meets, it seems.

Before leaving, he declared that he struggled to find opening words with strangers he might want to talk with. I recommended that he treat them without fear, taking on face value whatever reaction manifests, even if it is a curt rejection of connection. I am unsure if this was enough to help him talk more confidently now with others, but he is young and will clearly learn how to do this over time as I personally find him such an engaging fellow to talk with.

On a closer table to mine sat a family that I necessarily started talking with because all three offered calm smiles when I turned my attention to them. The boy was reading a book, which I endorsed of course. The girl was able to sit calmly throughout without recourse to the sating of a mobile phone addiction. Likewise the mother. All three were as calm of nature as their smiles.

Mother and son were visiting their daughter who is studying the oboe here in Cardiff. They had travelled from Wolverhampton, their Black Country accent quite alluring. The mother is a primary school teacher.

A gentle, easy chat with no exciting tales of coincidence to tell. In its own way, this is as appealing as the times when a synchronicity presents itself.

OCT 27 Arranged meeting with a stranger

Delon arranged for me to meet with **Lee**, a friend who might be able to help me with an alternative method of dealing with my anxiety and headaches. So I was meeting a stranger, yet in a sense not.

Alas, he proved to be a rather blunt man. He was learned but dismissed my declaration of twenty-five years of headaches as a failure to have an open heart. I tried to counter, but he seemed reluctant to shift opinion. He bombarded me with some fascinating and some scary matters, and I struggled to cope. I was being overwhelmed, denied the time I needed to reflect and ruminate on the many concepts he was throwing at me. Most certainly, this particular encounter with a stranger was one I was badly equipped to handle.

Delon remained a quiet observer – remarkably so. **Lee** insensitively *Welshified* his name by calling him *Dylan*. And this kind of summed up this stranger in my eyes – not able to empathise nor able to embrace a viewpoint that differed from his own.

I left very jaded and spent the rest of the day going through what he said. Most certainly there was great value in his advice, but it was hard to properly absorb because of the manner of delivery. Such situations in the past would have seen me well up with unavoidable tears. I can be a terribly sensitive creature at times.

OCT 28 — The warmest person I have met this year

I reflected with **Delon** on the meeting yesterday, and he apologised for the intensity I had to endure. **Lee** had changed recently, hardened, and this was something he felt he should have warned me about. **Delon** is always impeccable in manner and thought, so I of course declared no grudge.

I was still jaded, however, and had anxiety last night triggered by a strangely dry mouth. A chronic state of anxiety can amplify even minor ailments out of proportion. So I left Coffee #1 and sought advice in the Pharmacy next door. They assured me that it was nothing to worry about, cannot be treated and will go when the likely stress causing it goes.

So I was relieved and vastly lifted in mood. This was perfect because shortly after boarding a bus to go shopping, I observed an elderly lady walked into the bus with the most serene of natural smiles. She sat down behind me and I commented on that smile. We spoke briefly and then I faced forward for a while.

But the bus was very quiet and I turned around to mention this to her. She said that she liked to get out and meet people, and that most people she speaks with are nice. Her face was deeply lined, and I would guess she was in her eighties. I told her what I saw – that the lines were formed in a way that made a smile quite natural. And after a while, it crept up on me that she was like a cross between my warm and kindly mother and the same natured mother of an old school friend, the latter sharing the same Welsh accent and tenderness of word with this lady.

She was, I decided, the warmest person I have met in a very long time. There was something humble, gentle and caring about the way she spoke. I really want to meet her again for she soon disembarked, but not before I asked her name. **Queenie** she said! That was her real name, and her face lit up magnificently as she told me. She said that I had cheered her up and made her day. I wonder if more so than her effect on me? What an utter delight.

We waved goodbye to each other as the bus continued onwards.

Another book on thinking ...

Another day, another coffee shop. As I made my way to the window seat, I eyed a young man reading a large book, so asked on impulse how the book was. He had only read seventeen pages, but so far so good. **Matt** went on to say that it was a student chosen book for the 'A' level English Literature course that he teaches. He enthused about the concept of student- rather than teacher-centric study material, agreeing with me that ownership tends to help with understanding and engagement. And it also keeps the teacher on their toes and up to date.

    Matt was a delight to talk with. And to learn from. One technique he adopts is to teach via two concurrent books, each with a similar theme, with a view to comparing styles. For some reason or other, I decided that he might be interested in a copy of my *Think More* book. He said that he was indeed particularly interested in fact because it largely mirrors his own endeavours along the same lines. He sent me a copy of his book :

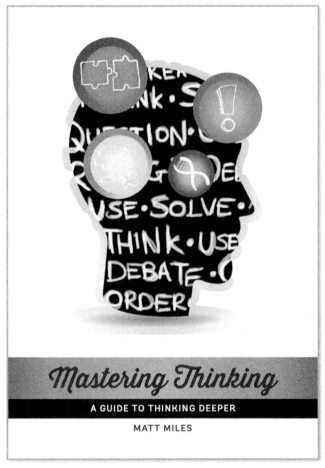

Last chat with Delon

Delon and I chatted for the last time before his departure to Portugal. A shame that such a great find, as it were, should be leaving. I have enjoyed the chats we have had, of course, but regret the chats we could have had that we no longer will. We can connect electronically, but face to face is an order of magnitude more enjoyable.

The obvious reasons why I find **Delon** so fascinating and intriguing to talk with are his enthusiasm, his energy, his broad knowledge base, and clarity of communication. But it is the more subtle aspect of his nature that is probably key – that he pauses and reflects on all that someone says to him, and delivers nuanced, holistic responses. They take me aback as they are so different from the *auto-pilot, shallow, predictable* replies that many people give. The difference is at once subtle, but also magnificently thought-provoking. I suspect that his years of Daoist training are at least part of this nature.

He kindly gave me some books to read as a parting gesture – *Factfulness* by Rosling and *Why* by Livio. The latter is subtitled *What makes us curious*, and this reflects very much a common theme **Delon** and I share.

Tried the Waterstones bookshop coffee shop in the afternoon. A young girl was running manically around so I spoke with her parents about channeling that energy into drama or dance. Strange that they were both as calm as their daughter was energised. Maybe parenting does that.

I met another mother of a hyper five year daughter on the bus later and asked that same question of her child (who incidentally was not present with the mother). This lady was cold and she let me hold her hand briefly as verification. Yup. Chilly fingers!

We talked the whole journey home, and it was clear that **Kirsty** was herself as high energy as her daughter. It was a great exercise in conversation skills to avoid being overloaded by her fast chat – some times I had to ask her to repeat what she said as the words were blurring into one long vocal mass. But she was fun. Scarily pale skinned, looking rather anaemic, she said that she did not have as much energy as she used to (wow!) and suspected insufficient B12 vitamins in her diet. She may well be right, but a little odd as she was a meat and poultry eater.

NOV 3 — Contact from Delon

Delon has today connected with me electronically courtesy of Facebook. He is settling in to a new life in Portugal. I told him how much I was enjoying the Daoist book he recommended, not least because it is written in a pragmatic style that is largely devoid of the elitism that can arise from mastering a fine skill.

NOV 6 — Persian smiles

Coffee #1 again. My reading now includes an intriguing book about *Alderian* psychology, where a key tenet is that you separate your tasks from others. So a child doing homework should own that task. Quite hard to see why a parent should not coerce or encourage rather than allow a child to neglect that task. But the narrative argues well. It is good to read different views on life even if you do not agree with them.

Whilst I sat in the window seat, three Persians sat nearby, replete with the most generous of smiles and manner. In particular, one of the two ladies had the kind of broad, deep smile that would make her prime candidate for a role in a *Wallace and Grommet* film made in flesh rather than with clay models. It was hard not to keep speaking with her so that I could keep seeing that smile spread right across her face.

NOV 7 — A tingling feeling!

Spoke with **Osman** in Coffee #1 this morning. Or to be more accurate, tried to. He has a more pronounced version of the machine-gun fire talking mode that I can slip into if not careful. The kind that asks a question but is so impatient for an answer that the next question is delivered before the other person has actually even started to reply to the first question.

So I suggested it would be wise for him to practice meditation and mindfulness. He was aware of these tools, but not sure where to start, so I gave him one of my books with guiding advice. He did say, however, that he is now attending yoga classes. I necessarily endorsed that enormously – training for mind, body and spirit is wonderful.

Later, just as I was leaving, a lady came in and asked if she could sit where he had sat. We chatted briefly, and it was like meeting **Osman**'s sister. Identical pace and nature of staccato speech. It was quite funny to see how similar she was to him, and he looked over with intrigue, maybe seeing that also. Her name was **Sue** and she too was receptive to the idea of meditation and mindfulness, and she too had just started a yoga course.

Lovely people but it is a little hard for me to stay calm of mind and mood when the speech of others seeks to solicit an equally fast stream of responses from myself.

First trip to Waterloo tea shop in a week after lunch. I sat inside in warm sun reading the Daoism book, with a most splendid view of autumn colours enflaming a tree nearby. A lady came in to buy some cakes and take photos of one of the paintings on the wall. I asked her if she too was an artist, and yes, she was, using the same *acrylic-pouring-onto-canvas* style as the painting she was photographing. She seemed happy to chat, with a little caution in her voice and manner. Clearly, she was a caring, sensitive person.

But as we spoke, we both became energised and discovered that we shared a sensitive nature that lead to anxiety problems. She ended her academic degree early because of panic attacks. She is now a worker with adults with learning difficulties. I just noticed the second 'f' on that word 'difficulties' fuses with the 'i', and omits the dot above it. Such sensitivity to detail and feelings is something I discussed with her as being at the root of anxiety problems. We sensitive types can overload easily.

Her name was **Fiona**, and after maybe ten or fifteen minutes of talking, I had to tell her that I felt a kind of tingling mix of anxiety and excitement from our chat and connection. Her face by now was so amazingly animated that it made me feel even more affected. A chemistry that I have not felt even close to feeling with another human this year. In fact, maybe never. And she seemed to feel the same. I guessed rightly that she is a vegan. She has joined *Extinction Rebellion* because of how passionately she feels about the many things that are deeply wrong about the world. One thing I mentioned nearly solicited tears. Not in a clumsy way, but simply because she felt the injustice in the story I was relating.

She too felt that the world was a connected place, and loves talking with strangers. She implied that there was a sense of pre-destiny about our encounter today.

I gave her a copy of *Improve your life* and she was delighted, saying that it was a particularly salient time to read such a book. We shook hands. Twice, and she departed with a beaming smile.

It is hard to explain in words what is experienced personally. They need to be felt, but rarely are as a result of just hearing words. We feel what others feel with a shallow sentiment that is hard to overcome.

I do not think I will forget the tingling feeling talking with **Fiona**. It cannot be repeated – its transience in part is what will makes it special in my memory. The contrast with recent intense and sustained bouts of anxiety is palpable.

NOV 8 Social media policy advisor

As I waited for a top up of my pot of tea in Coffee #1, I found myself stood near a tall lady with a resplendent mane of wavy hair, deeply engrossed in the activity of tracing her thumb around her mobile phone screen. So I asked her, probably a little too confrontationally, if she was always glued to her phone. She was entirely unfazed by my question and had a most excellent reply to offer. Each weekend, she has a personal embargo on phone use from 6pm Saturday to 8am Monday. It took her *six weeks* to get used to this and realised as a consequence how truly addicted she had been to her phone. By contrast, my normal phone use is ten minutes each morning doing brain training and a few checks in the day to see what is happening on the WhatsApp pages for the tennis club at the end of my road.

She said it was important that she use her phone a great deal as she is a social media policy advisor. How cool is that! She used to work in the Home Office in London, at the time of the Grenfell fire disaster. I asked her if she found the Conservative Home Office staff callous. Her reply was to see the word as far too soft. The atmosphere was so caustic, so toxic, that she escaped and now works for the Welsh Government.

NOV 9 Piano hands

I was sat in Coffee #1 on a Saturday morning, waiting to chat with my sister and nephew, when a mother and two teenage daughters sat nearby. One of these girls was exquisitely pretty with an elegance about her poise and movement that was deeply fascinating to observe. I had slept really well and my mind was really receptive to subtleties. Her slender fingers lifted her cup of tea with an embrace, a delicacy of touch that I so rarely ever seen.

I was compelled to ask her if she was a piano player, first engaging eye contact with her mother as a kind of unspoken permission to speak with a junior. The girl smiled and said that yes, she did play piano. A Bach piece was her favourite. Alas, she had not played any Debussy yet. Her face lit up as she spoke, with symmetric dimples emerging as she did so. Quite delightful, as if she had been transported from a country house in the Victorian era, even if necessarily dressed in modern clothes.

NOV 11 Dyfed Cynan

A long, deeply restful night of sleep combined with a gym session to see me bounding with energy into Coffee #1 and no hope therefore for the poor man in front of me to queue in peace! He was, however, most delightfully accommodating. A man of rare warmth and generosity of nature. And patience for permitting me to ask why he had no socks on! I asked because he was wrapped up very warmly yet had bare ankles. It seem incongruous. I discovered that **Dyfed Cynan** is an English/Welsh actor, a very 'pretty' man and a delight to talk with.

NOV 12 Iqos

I talked with another Coffee #1 customer and discovered that he worked for Philip Morris who I knew were in the tobacco business. He declared that he used to smoke but no longer does. So I was necessarily curious about his role in the company. He now works on user liaison (I think he said) on a new venture that has been ten years in the making at the cost of billions. The new product is called *Iqos*. Straddling the gap between cigarette smoking and vaping, it offers a tobacco product that is heated rather than burnt, thereby avoiding the carcinogenic of the latter. Remarkably it claims to reduce by 95% the harmful effects of tobacco use.

As a non-smoker, I might never have encountered this new venture at this stage. Apparently there is an Iqos shop in Cardiff city centre. Will have a look in but have never smoked and never intend to (apart from one puff aged eleven on the field adjacent the school playing field in London. The combination of abrasive texture and cost deterred me for life).

Yoga teacher

I asked the lady in the comfy chair by the window in Coffee #1 this morning if I could sit in the adjacent chair. You see the pattern here. But it is an easy way to meet strangers. Dressed in autumn colours, with wavy hair equally seasonal in colour, she was happy for me to sit there. But because my sore throat was affected by speech, I had no intention of any sustained chatting.

But it was impossible not to do so with **Lou** for she was a rare character. A declared empath, yoga teacher and also a lifetime sufferer of anxiety. She was a little flat of mood now because she was shocked at the state of the nation, returning recently from ten years spent living in India where she also taught yoga amongst other things. She studiously avoided the media for mental health reasons. She attended long retreats in silence. A very spiritual woman, **Lou** was engaging of expression as well as of word, her face animated by a similar child-like excitement that lit up mine.

After a while, she disappeared to have *Eye Movement Desensitisation and Reprocessing (*EMDR) treatment for her anxiety. This is new to me – I hope I see her again to hear of the outcome, and to resume our conversation.

Students

There are some regular students in Coffee #1 in Wellfield Road. Some descend from a nearby sixth form college during 'free' lesson slots. One I see regularly was on his own today so I spoke with him. He said that he was studying economics as one of his 'A' levels, and this lead to a shared voicing of approval of socialism and an anger at Neoliberalism. It was an easy, energised, informed chat, this young man clearly articulate as well as able to smile a lot. So it is as surprising as it is upsetting to discover that **Matt** has dyslexia, and suffers from anxiety and depression. I gave him one of my books to read, hopefully to help a little.

The bus into town later was nearly full with students so I had to ask to sit next to one in almost the only empty seat I could see. She was from Iran and during our chat I had to declare, to her amusement, but also her understanding, that at age eighteen she was more mature than myself. Very calm and measured in her speech and entirely open to anything that I cared to talk about. She did say that she remained calm unless pushed and pushed and pushed when she would then boil over. I told her that this must be greeted with surprise for she was the pinnacle of calm to me.

NOV 18 Reading in the park

The sunshine lured me into a walk around Roath Park and its lake. It was a day blessed with wall to wall blue sky, and on the way home I sat on a bench to read underneath that canopy. A couple walking past stopped to speak. Not to say empty hellos, but to connect. It is extremely rare for anyone to do that when I am sat reading. The lady, with that familiar disarming, warm *Essex* accent proclaimed how good an idea it was to do what I was doing. To take their reading habit to the park just as I was. Her husband was equally chatty and relaxing of manner, his warm nature originating from Derbyshire. They were clearly supremely well matched personalities.

We talked about the wonderful libraries we have in Cardiff, and I mentioned a talk about anxiety this week in the branch near me. And she then revealed that she suffers with this condition – yet it seemed impossible that such a relaxed lady should do so. She was terribly grateful when I gave her a copy of *Improving your life.* She made a point of ensuring there was a way to feedback to me. What a lovely couple.

At the Plasnewydd Community centre this evening, I bumped into a stranger. She was asking where the Writer's class was in the building. I had no idea, but I asked her about this, saying also that I was a writer. **Louise** was excited to meet a fellow author. It transpired that she was in the wrong community centre, but suggested I join the group some time.

I later found **Louise** on Facebook, sending her a message. Then I noticed that we had a shared friend, **Shaughan-'sniffer'-Feakes.** This is a little bizarre as I used to play in the same BBC football team in the 1970's and 1980's with **Shaughan** (nicknamed for his ability to sniff out goal opportunities). He moved to Cardiff a few years ago.

NOV 21 TV locations manager

Waterloo tea shop sits in a well-to-do part of Cardiff, attracting many middle and upper class 'clientele'. So it was no huge surprise that I should encounter a lady working in *TV production*. Her name was **Jess** and she was looking to sit down, so I invited her to sit in one of the armchairs opposite the sofa I was sat on, with the intention of making the chat brief, because she had a laptop and needed to work. I waited until the conversation reached a pause to let her work. But she kept talking and intriguing me. She looked business like but was very warm of word. A most fascinating conversation we had, daisy-chaining in true ADHD fashion on the slightest cue from subject to subject. **Jess** was a TV locations manager who also had ADHD.

I mentioned to her how the girl screaming in the tea shop was actually painful to my ears. She agreed and said that she also suffered with *misphonia*, the term for an oversensitivity to sounds. For **Jess** it was especially sneezes, which is precisely one of my most hated problems! No matter what I am doing, no matter how relaxed I am, the sound of someone sneezing will flood my mind and I will feel a kind of anger in accord with the angry aggression of the sneeze. It is desperately frustrating as it coerces me to really, really want to tell the person not to be annoying me with that horrible sneeze sound. But that would be quite socially unacceptable. Irrational to the eyes of those not afflicted by this condition. The odd thing is that **Jess** seemed to be too easy going a person to be likewise afflicted.

At one point, as I returned to my book, I overheard her talk on the phone with the producer or director of a dramatisation of the Salisbury *Novichok* poisoning incident. She had declared an endless frustration with the disorganisation of TV film crews, the impact upon herself heavy at times as they regularly failed to give her enough notice to acquire filming rights. This was especially a problem in Salisbury as the residents really did not want a film crew to open old wounds, as it were.

A very different life from mine – having to plan ahead a great deal to ensure continuity of work. Such is the nature of many of the arts.

NOV 23   Derek

To town on the bus on yet another dreary, dull, wet day. A young man sat down near me at the back, and I said hello. **Derek** was a Ugandan student studying for a Masters degree in material science. As I always do, I asked him what the thesis was. He said it was an exploration of a leading edge advance in concrete technology that he described as 'self-healing'. Naturally, I was curious, and he explained that capsules containing bacteria are randomly distributed through the material. When a fracture starts, it bursts the capsule and the released bacteria spreads into the fissure and heal it. At least in theory.

He was a very warm, friendly and relaxed fellow, making a rather slow bus journey most enjoyable. I asked him where he was headed, and **Derek** said that he needed to catch a second bus to Coryton for a part time job. Now this was most interesting as his job was quite different from the academic world of his degree. But he was equally excited. He worked as a carer, with many of his 'clients' (how I hate that modern label) suffering with mental health problems. He made a point of saying how good this job was to teach him to 'open himself out'. It is not so often that someone I meet couples compassion with a technical mind. Most fascinating.

He also made a point, unsolicited, that Britain was so much more organised than Uganda, his home country. Here, **Derek** said that you could check on the internet when a bus would be leaving, go to the bus stop and catch that bus pretty much on time. In Uganda, this would be unlikely. Everyone there, he declared, tended to do their own thing, so coordinated efforts were pretty rare. Clearly a generalisation but still quite chilling if only a half truth.

NOV 24 The most sociable of brothers

Sunday mornings I nearly always see two families that meet for coffee in Coffee #1. To feel a little bit connected to them is nice and grounding. But there was no sign of them today. Instead, two brothers came in and sat without the accompaniment of parents. These were no ordinary boys, but supremely engaging, socially adept beings. Remarkably so considering that they were only eleven and twelve years of age.

We talked about many things, not least the younger boy's dyspraxia and how mindfulness is helping him handle life. But their enthusiasm, energy, wonderfully eloquent articulations, politeness and sheer curiosity were breathtaking. It was like talking to mature adults in a way. Clearly their parents were facilitating, encouraging, smart people. One parent ran a hostel for homeless people.

The elder boy proclaimed that he loved non-fiction books, avoided being tied to his mobile phone, was deep into maths and science, but, delightfully, also loved being creative. Since they both also played chess, I gave them a copy of a compendium of some of my books. It teaches Go and has an array of diverse topics.

Now here is the nature of these boys. Each, in turn, came over to shake my hand in thanks for the book. And it was patently clear that this was from the heart, and not some mechanical gesture because the younger boy then insisted on taking a selfie of him and I to show his parents. This felt rather awkward, but I felt I should oblige.

Naturally, I am deeply curious about the nature of their parents – what people were able to help their young develop such advanced and balanced social skills? To be so vibrantly alive!

I realised that I actually felt less confident talking with these boys than they did with me. Seriously. I am a seasoned, well travelled talker, yet was being upstaged by these boys.

Postscript – in hindsight, the next day I realised that they were probably friends rather than brothers. I presumed the latter as they were so much in accord in outlook and social development.

NOV 29 Alan

This most miserable of Novembers came to life, at last, and I was fortunate to get a comfy chair in the window of Waterloo tea shop, where I sat bathed in warm sunshine reading my latest books. One of these by Peter Marren is entitled 'Mushrooms'. Except that it is a book about fungi also, since the mushrooms are merely the fruit of the fungi. And what, might you think, is particularly interesting about fungi?

First, that fungi are neither plant not animal. They have their own kingdom. And the diversity of fungi and their fruits is immense and utterly beguiling. Some species play a vital role supplying nutrients in the soil to the roots of trees, in turn receiving sugars the trees create in their leaves. The trees are actually incapable of extracting these nutrients from the soil. (And did you ever wonder how trees nourished themselves in the winter when all the leaves have fallen? I simply do not know).

As I read, a man entered the shop and immediately came to me to declare that I had the best spot in the whole place. He was a friendly fellow, and obvious to conclude this, I suspect, as very few people actually volunteer connections with middle aged strangers such as myself.

His accent was familiar, so I asked. You guessed, he used to live in Stoke Newington in London where I lived for a few years in my BBC days. Like me, he did not support a local team, preferring to follow Wolverhampton Wanderers instead. We had a nice chat about football. He asked my name, so I discover that his is **Alan**.

A splendid fellow.

A fellow sufferer

I passed a lady on the way back to my seat in Coffee #1 this Saturday morning. She looked relaxed, smiling sweetly as she looked up from her book as I walked by. Of course, I asked about the book and saw that the cover looked like a love story. The title "I said I loved you" gave clue to that. But it was non-fiction, she told me, relating the handling of depression by the author. She too had suffered depression to the point where she was actually hospitalised. I felt desperately sorry for her but wanted to keep the chat light and not overbearing or serious. I shared my own dabbling with depression, anxiety and the like.

Her name was **Louise** and I felt it more than prudent to give her a copy of my self-help book, and she in turn recommended that I read "An unquiet mind". She said that she was hyper-sensitive in nature, affected by all the detail around her, especially the feelings of others. Clearly a far greater empath than myself. But as she spoke, she was quite energised, but her appearance was momentarily flecked with face *droops* as if depression always wanted to express itself even if for just a fraction of time. I noticed that in addition to a beguiling smile, she was beautiful. Not sure why I only now noticed this, but I immediately told her so. I told her also that I like to do this in earnest rather than to flatter. She too does the same! She tells others around her of the beauty they carry with them, by looks or apparel.

I asked her if she wrote, and yes, thousands or articles! Many on the matter of *synchronicity* also! I offered to help her publish to Amazon. It is such a nice feeling to try to help someone when the effort of doing is so trivial when compared to the potential benefit. Hopefully I will see and speak to her again.

Still I get caught out by the judgement trap!

Whilst sat reading in the comfy chair by the window in Coffee #1 today, a lady hovered nearby. She cautiously asked if she could sit down to have coffee before going to her hairdresser's appointment. Like myself, the lady was retired, but quite differently from I, she spoke with a gentle, soft, warm voice. I did not return to my book because we embarked on an *understated* kind of conversation. Low-key it may have been, but still most pleasant in large part because of her gentle demeanour. From Surrey, **Angela** had to admit that she had to work at her calm – she was not like this when younger.

Later in the day I found myself at the top front of a double decker bus gliding and stumbling through roads sprinkled with sunlight trees. Two young ladies sat on the front seat after a while and I nearly greeted them with the Arabic for 'Peace be with you'. They were black haired with tanned skin, heavy makeup and elongated eyelashes. I had presumed, utterly falsely, that they were speaking Arabic.

How wrong was I?

Embarrassingly *very* wrong for they were visiting from Sweden! They were easy to talk with but they sadly had to admit that not everyone in Sweden was able to chat as they were. Many were endlessly, addictively absorbed in their mobile phones, just as here the UK. They described the situation as two classes of people, and those phone-bound really did struggle with face-to-face conversation. Very sad.

DEC 4 — Open-hearted awareness

Sometimes my reading gets stuck. Bogged down, so that I am no longer absorbing the meaning. This happened with the book "Shift into freedom : The science and practice of open-hearted awareness" so I decided to start-over after reading as far as page fifty-five first time through.

It is a book teaching us to return to a pure and simple state *awareness*, on the premise that it has been pushed away by a focus on *what* we are aware of. We get caught up in doing life but can step back into awareness that is free from ego, thought and emotion. I mention this book in part because of some commentary within it that relates to my journey :

> *Awake awareness is invisible, contentless, formless, boundless and timeless, but is the ground of our being. When you shift out of your conventional sense of self, there is a gap of not-knowing. Awake awareness of who we **are** prior to the personal conditioning we usually turn to for our identity.*

> *We begin to move from open-mindedness to **open-hearted awareness**, where the expression of awake awareness then knows unconditional love and interconnectedness with all things.*

This is rather hard to grasp, but I do often find myself detached from a sense of self when engaging in conversation with a stranger. I project into them and kind of *become them* retaining a distinct awareness of this process. An awareness born out of excitement of the process.

DEC 6 Conversations with three Christians

It seems that I meet a disproportionate number of Christians in my travels and Coffee shop residencies. Today it was a sequence of three such people, and what a delight it was.

I sat in an upstairs comfy chair for a change and immediately engaged in conversation with the man sat at the table in the window. His laptop was open and curiosity got the better of me. He said that he was writing an essay on two gospels from the bible. How they related to each other. I mentioned that **Talia** was doing a year long Christian leadership course, and this triggered conversation about the nature of leadership. My mind jumped to the most extreme of bad leaders, Donald Trump and how power often attracts precisely the wrong types. He described how this pattern unfolded when he worked in the local council. One man in particular was egocentrically driven, un-empathic in the extreme, hell-bent on rising up the ladder fast. They wanted to stop him making the wrong decisions, so sought a way to derail him. They realised, quite sagely, that he presumed, true to his egocentric nature, that other people would think exactly as he did. So they hatched a plan that avoided the obvious route he thought they would take.

Shortly after this interesting fellow left his table, a lady arrived very heavily clothed and sat on another table near to me. It was a mild day so I asked her why all the clothes. She was happy to talk, beaming a smile at me and explaining how she had a sore neck and wanted to keep it very warm. And we kept talking.

Her name was **Samantha Nagtegaal** and she was a true delight to engage with. A deeply warm, caring, creative, sensitive, expressive, curious type. I am not sure there are any character boxes that I love that she did not tick. She could talk as much as I but was fascinating to listen to. For five years, she has been running the *CookingForSanity.com* web site, one of the few creative outlets being a mother that was permitted her. I gave her a colour copy of my recent *Eclectic* book – a collection of pictures and writings. It seemed that she was the perfect audience, and I was pleased that she was excited to receive it.

Another Christian, she talked also of difficulties with her nine year old son, and that autism might explain his struggles, so they are looking to request a diagnosis. I explained that I was personally most likely to be on the spectrum, so gave some ideas to try to help her both understand autism and enable the good things that can manifest from this *nature*.

She declared that she was an extrovert, but I was very suspicious and told her so. There were many times where she needed more time to think about things than were possible. A sign that thinking and reflection, introversion activities, were vital to her life. At least I got her to ponder upon this matter.

She seemed to be bursting with life from our conversation. I was a little tired and heady, but managed to share her enthusiasm. I mentioned how I was using the game of Go to add to my meditations, and she then said that her interest in Japanese Anime had brought the game to her attention. She had watched the excellent *Hikaru No Go* anime series about a boy who is guided to play Go to a high level by the spirit of an ancient master of the game (as depicted in the splendid picture on the next page). The video was produced by the Japanese Go Association to try to encourage more Japanese youngsters to play the game. It actually succeeded in getting more players all around the world involved as the series was an International success.

I was getting quite tired, and my tea was nearly all used up when **Talia** happened to walk in. Of course, I had to introduce her to **Sam**. And the three of us had a chat for a good half an hour, although for once I did most of the listening. The energy levels here were great – these two ladies connected immediately and it was more than enough for me to just listen in.

When **Sam** left, I chatted with **Talia** a while longer. I was really getting headachy but she was regaling dialogues she was having with God in such a lucid fashion that I just had to stay and listen further. She sees things with such a detailed understanding. The kind of forensic level of mental clarity that scientists need, yet **Talia** is not an academic type at all. It is most odd.

I was pretty jaded by the time I got home. Tired from a sustained period of concentration talking and listening. But it was OK as I was infused with a feeling of completeness and grounding that the connections gave me.

Ever smiling Tessa

It was trivially easy to make friends with **Tessa**, a new member of the Coffee #1 staff in Wellfield Road. She has blond hair, and blue eyes that radiate like beacons. An immensely natural, expressive but empathic lady, she is fun and effortless to chat with and tolerates with remarkable equanimity my frequent anecdotes and childish quips (although I do really try to be meaningful).

She was aware of the writing of this book and the encounters that I have had, so implored me to read about *ethnography* – a branch of sociology. I believe that **Tessa** studied anthropology. I asked her if she could find a best newbies book on the subject. Now, as you might guess, I am intrigued.

Four chats

The same routine four days a week for fifteen months now is to strengthen my leg muscles in the gym, followed by tea in Coffee #1. Had a lovely chat with a new lady in the gym from Derbyshire. An English 'A' level teacher and also a hypnotherapist with a son who has high functioning autism. Such chats make time in the gym fly by, but my fitness efforts are then somewhat reduced ...

Sat next to another new lady in the coffee shop. **Meg** was on a day off work and happy to chat for half an hour. She works in Admin at the University but is clearly a tad too bright to do just that so 'digresses' into areas outside of her remit. She is a very easy going lady who recently had sleep anxiety so read lots of books on the subject because this anxiety was pretty much alien to her. This lead her to attending a counselling course where she learned greatly about the navigation of social situations. One matter that struck a nerve with her was that we cannot change other people since they must first want to change themselves. So our responsibility towards them is something we often try too hard at and can therefore ease back on.

I offered her one of my books to read and she selected the one on thinking. I wonder if she will let me know her thoughts?

Mid afternoon, rain pounding down from grey clouds, I took the bus to Waitrose. I sat facing a young man with long but wavy blonde hair. He was listening to music so I probably should not have interrupted him. But I was driven to tell him that I liked his hair. He was more than happy to remove his earpieces and thank me. You might guess next that I asked him if he was in a band. He was. Was he a drummer? Yes. How cool!

A true delight to talk to, animated and happy to discuss his band **Wyllt** (I think I recall the name correctly), best pronounced rather sharply, the soft double-L preceding a strong T. He said that they were a slow, deep metallic band, and I came up with a lame choice of band from my past as an example I knew; Black Sabbath; knowing that they were only partly metallic. But I discovered from him that it was this very band that kick started the metallic movement. He felt that "Sabbath, bloody Sabbath" was their best album. I mentioned how good the drummer was in *The Sweet* and he agreed, saying that he had previously been in the band *Yes* which he adored. **Shaun** was a delight to talk with, shaking my hand as he left the bus.

I sat at the high bench to drink my tea in Waitrose shortly after this, and recognised the elderly lady on my right after a few minutes talking with her. "You are the lady with cold hands", I declared, and she was most happy that I remembered this. They were, again, most cold to the touch. She talked with greater animation and verve this time, especially when recounting some children she taught English to who declared they were 'too thick' to understand poetry. So she made it come alive as much as possible. For one war poem, she arranged for the children to visit a war museum where the latin title of the poem was on a plaque underneath a war scene. It thrilled these children. And as she was recounting this story, her eyes started reddening a little and welling up with tears. I was, in effect, honoured that someone might share something that meant so much in such a tender way.

Now I know her name is **Pam**, but she suggested to me to remember it as rhyming with ham. She told me a story that I think (not always hearing each word she said as she was quietly spoken) was about being mindful of simple acts as brushing your teeth. She was asked by the instructor what she thought of when brushing, expecting her to say that her mind wandered off relatively randomly. Instead, **Pam** said that she always remembered to brush the four *quadrants* of her mouth, on the *lingual* and *palatal* sides. She seemed to feel this was common parlance, but I told her that it was the first time I had heard these terms.

I gave her a copy of my short novel, with a vibrant butterfly picture on the cover. A risky exposure to an English teacher, but she was happy to receive it.

Drummer boy

I did it again! A boy of around sixteen years of age was walking towards me on my way home from Waterloo tea shop patting the front of his jacket where maybe a book or other bulky object was pressed inside. I immediately asked him if he was a drummer and yup, I was right again. Much to his bemusement.

The tea shop supplied some little chats, not least with a lady in a dark pink coat that I described to her as fuchsia in colour (how mad the spelling of that word is – how perverse our language). She was happy to chat but mostly happy because she had herself been looking for that word to describe that particular shade of pink.

But most of all, I enjoyed reading from the book that **Tessa** had recommended. "Watching the English" by Kate Fox is a classic ethnographic or anthropologic primer. Near six hundred pages going into the minutiae of our quirky behaviour. I must quote from the book as it is clear even in the first sixty pages that I break a lot of the 'rules'. Kate talks of a default 'question' we often use when passing someone we know. We say "How are you" but it is more a grooming *opener* than a real question. She says :

> *The automatic, ritual response is "Fine, thanks", "OK, thanks", "Oh, mustn't grumble"*

> *If you are terminally ill, it is acceptable to say "Not bad, considering"*

All of this serving to illustrate the overly cautious, awkward, tip-toeing game we feel obliged to pursue to avoid the dreaded taboo of saying the wrong thing. It rarely serves us too well so I try to be much more forward, albeit tempering my forwardness with an upbeat, humoured tone.

The fruit and vegetable stall holder I pass each time I go to the gym now has his brother working for him. He frequently makes very funny comments about my unseasonal wearing of shorts. A few days ago he asked my name and then laughed when I said it because he too was called Neil.

It is so nice to be friendly with this Neil as he is like a Scouser – always joking around without that joking being vindictive. A benign sense of humour, a naturally generous and sociable nature. He was fascinated when I told him about this book. Will try to remember to give him a copy.

DEC 17 Amy and Dexter

When is a stranger no longer a stranger? Is it when they are familiar by appearance, even if you have not spoken with them? Or do you have to chat to connect with them to declare them to be friend or acquaintance now?

I smiled at the little boy of a lady I saw from time to time. Both he and her would smile back. Before I eventually spoke to her, were the smiles enough to stop them being strangers?

They were sat at the window table in Coffee #1, his eyes beaming with life, inciting the same in his mother. **Amy** said that she never had truly wanted children but the child she has now is so remarkable. Clearly content and happy in his own skin – even though today he was struggling with a cold. Before I left, they had a laughter infused 'fight' on the shop floor. The normal British inhibitions of social behaviour gone – but what delight!

Amy wants to address the thorny issue that bugs me – where some young people have such stymied social skills, face to face communication being beyond some of them she says. She might join the police force, although they have far too little time or task to deal with childhood social awkwardness issues. But nice for me to meet someone who shared in my strong concern about the instant gratification, entitlement and other issues that can and do damage the development of children.

Rather off-message, but certainly in the synchronicity bracket, I decided to contact *IPSO*, the British newspaper regulatory body regarding their Editors' code of practice document. I was referred to the web site for the setters of that code.

I sent an email to the secretary, **Jonathan Grun**, and realised after seeing his photo that he looked familiar. He replied that he was indeed in my brother's class at Howardian on the 1970's. He even knew me via my 2005 Cardiff Pubs web site venture. Alas, he offered obfuscation in reply to inquiry regarding the omission of definitions of the newspaper permitted *editorialising* and *campaigning* terms. Why, I wanted to know, were character assassinations endlessly deployed against Jeremy Corbyn deemed to be part of a campaign? Normally, newspaper campaigns are about saving people in need or protecting the environment. These attacks were pure *propaganda*.

I digress. These connections with people can materialise even when you really are not expecting them. They remain as funny to me as they are curious.

Microchatting

A fascinating morning with a sprinkling of little chats. Discussed the impeachment of Donald Trump with two men in the gym before catching the bus to Waitrose. Had a brief exchange of words with I believe a Middle Eastern man sat next to me before he left – he seemed surprised that I should then wish him a good day. At the tea/coffee bar in Waitrose, the middle aged lady to my right was most happy to chat. Her name was **Pamela**, (another *Pam*) and she seemed to be completely on my wavelength when I talked about the problem we humans have with leaders. That we seem to allow a stream of people to take power who we would not trust getting a round of drinks in. Why do we see the ability to talk at ease and with confidence in front of groups of people as the sole arbitrating factor in the leader selection process? She said that she shops here every Thursday and would love to meet again. How nice is that!

The young lady at the checkout was very bubbly of nature. Asked if she was a student she said that her path was very much not the University one, instead having studied horse management. I mentioned that my cousin had a lifelong love of these grand creatures, even though they made her eczema flair up badly. This lady in front of me had the exact same passion and problem. Maybe it is a common malady for equine lovers?

At the bus stop waiting for the bus home, a young man appeared dressed in rebellious fashion, a kind of cross between punk and motorbike rider. One of the patches sewn into his clothes was for the band *Black Sabbath*. You can guess he was a musician, a guitar player for eighteen years now (he was seven when he started) but not yet able to find a good enough band to join. I asked him if he knew *Uriah Heap*, a great band from the seventies. Immediately he said that he was listening to them yesterday! How connected I feel in such chats, in spite of a thirty-seven year age gap between him and I.

On the way home, I sat on the top front seat on the bus, even if the rain-splattered scenery outside was dull to behold, alas, so I started a conversation with another front seat passenger. A marketer and negotiator for a firm of accountants formerly owned by his father. He lamented how often payments for work, sometimes in the region of hundreds of thousands of pounds were delayed as long as nine months in some cases. The trend for payment delay a signature of an uncaring and unethical culture in the business world. I was tensing up in the chat when this fellow repeated how the head office of these accountants in Leeds wanted him to relocate there, so I got off two stops early to start the process of un-tensing.

I walked straight to Coffee #1 for a latte, a good remedy for a poorly head. Yup, more indulgence. **Ed** the environmentalist was in the queue ahead of me so I talked heatedly about the extreme Australian heatwave now that is wiping vast swathes of greenery from the land. And we got to talking about Trump's impeachment as we queued, which made the man ahead of **Ed** turn around to add his own views, with a lovely smirky smile on his face.

Josephine spotted me as I sat in the conservatory to read, and chatted a while. A Spanish man with a Japanese anime cartoon book sat down after a while. A resident here for a dozen years or so, his accent had mutated somewhat. I recommended that he visit Japan if at all possible, and he said that it was indeed in his plans, not least as one of his relations lives there and some day soon he will need to 'pop over' there. I reminded him that the flight alone was twelve hours ...

Before leaving, I chatted with a Psychology PhD student sat cross legged and bare armed on a sofa. Very pretty and very open to conversation. Her name was **Molly** and she seemed deeply thrilled to hear of some anecdotes from this book. She is working on the psychology of sleep, but has not yet determined the nature of the thesis itself. Quite remarkably, she said to me that it would be nice to talk again. I am unsure how to understand this, but suspect that she is simply a great connector.

On the way home, the owner of a nearby Chinese restaurant stopped me to talk about the central heating *and* deep freezer problems she is having. It was almost as if I wore a sign on my head that said "Talk to me".

Further along, a neighbour also stopped to enlighten me about her own precarious plight. But it was nice to connect with all these people. A life reaffirming experience.

DEC 22 · My friendly neighbours

Early today, a neighbouring family walked towards me. The girl, **Afnan** did not, however. Instead she ran forwards with a big grin on her face. She had left her house to post a Christmas card to me but now saw me approaching by chance. Such a nice gesture from a girl aged about six years.

DEC 23 — Mental health therapist

I was sat in Coffee #1 when a fresh faced young man walks in to sit near me. I soon discover that he works in Hillingdon in West London where I was born. As an NHS mental health therapist, I felt obliged to trot out the nature of the stats on that profession – that cuts had increased delays and created a critical bed shortage. In response, his key bugbear was that 'straight forward' matters such as anxiety and depression, the response is particularly rapid and effective, but in chronic cases such as bipolar and psychosis, where the ongoing support was vital, he said that the sufferers were frequently let down. And that the net effect was a greater cost on the NHS as the consequences had to be picked up by the police and A&E services. Cuts to mental health provision were maddeningly false savings.

On the way home I bumped into a tennis club friend. Not a stranger now, but I mention him because this was the first time we had met outside the tennis club and he chose to break the social 'safe distance' for talking. His face was about six inches from mine. I chose to observe my emotional reaction that was impelling me to pull back and get stressed, and just let it be. My emotions calmed and we chatted nicely. Challenge habits!

DEC 27 — Loud lady

On the bus to Waitrose on this grey, dank day, I found myself strangely mesmerised by the bare trees as they sped past outside. After knowing for a very long time that I was lucky to have extremely good eyesight, I now relish being able to see the fine tracery of twigs and branches, even on distant trees. But my meditations were unsettled by a loud lady who came onto the bus and sat near me. Talking fiercely about her phones and swearing in a chat on one of them, she seemed to behave as if alone, not in a public space.

I wondered why I can get irritated by such people. Is it that they sound annoying, or is it that I lose a sense of control of my environment? Or that the next 'noise' was unpredictable? My feeling inside was ugly in comparison to the calm of my trees absorption. But I did not want to feel bad. And I realised if I told her off for swearing unnecessarily she would like 'react'.

She asked the driver if the bus was stopping near the hospital – my stop also. Impulsively, before we arrived, I told her that her stop was the one after the next. She gave me a particularly sweet thanks and my mood immediately lifted. How simple was that?

Later in the day on the high street I observed a rarity – a person using their mobile phone but not actually walking. She was near my age and I mentioned to her how rare this was. She said that she had to stop because if she typed whilst walking she got dizzy!

DEC 29 — Angela and Sarah

Sunday morning and the threat of actual, real sunshine! So I sat in the window seat upstairs in Coffee #1 in keen anticipation. A lady sat near gave me a very relaxed smile, and I forgot my new rule of not trying to guess accents. You will realise why when I say that I guessed that this Cardiff girl, named **Angela**, was Australian. Doh! Her friend, **Sarah** returned to sit with her but she *was* in fact Australian. Maybe some of her accent had rubbed off in conversation, but whatever, they were charming to talk with, conversation shifting from the extreme heat in Australia to tennis at the David Lloyd centre, where **Angela** plays. No less that fifty one ladies in their WhatsApp group – when I put a message out on the group for my tennis club I rarely get a single taker. Double Doh!

At the tennis courts later I spotted a friend, **Mo**, having a gentle rally with two boys. He tells me they are his cousins, although they look like miniature versions of him, but with bigger smiles. These are special young people, so full of vitality and so clearly very alert and bright, ten and eleven years old. The elder stopped to talk with me and I sensed enormous energy of mind. I asked him if he was a deep thinker. He agreed but was puzzled how I knew. It was clear, I said, because most people respond automatically in conversation whereas he obviously deliberated first.

DEC 30 — Blue sky day

A rare day of brilliant blue sky. But first, to the gym where a new woman appeared. I spoke with her and discovered she was younger than appeared. "You're a schoolgirl?" I asked incredulously. She said that many thought she was older than she was. A delight to talk with, warm and naturally sociable, she was contemplating either French at University or a path into drama, but felt inclined to take the safer first route. She admitted that this important decision was thrust upon teenagers too early in their lives.

Late morning in the Castle grounds, a lady was crouching down to take a photograph of her partner, and doing so as if she was using a professional camera rather than a mobile phone. I offered to take a photograph of the two of them and briefly chatted. They were in their twenties and genuinely warm and friendly to me, a complete stranger. From Turkey, I pondered what connection with that country I could offer. But all that came to mind was the Galatasaray football team. And Istanbul where Liverpool won the Champions League in 2005. But I did not and made a mental note of learning more about Turkey some time.

At Waterloo tea shop in the afternoon, **Beth** a primary school teacher and **Chris**, an associate physician asked to sit on the outside table with me along with their snow white Alsatian. They were also a pleasure to talk with, both saying how they loved their jobs, clearly caring, empathic people. So I had to ask how he handled the need to be empathic and caring with the emotional overload that can result from doing his job. He said that he feels the emotions, such as when a patient describes a poorly state of health, but then lets that be replaced by an action, a response. Crucially, he said that he reflected on these emotions later in the day. I said to **Beth** that there was a parallel in education where lessons are indeed not learn until consolidated at night – poor sleep can badly compromise that process.

When their cake and scone arrived, the dog started to become agitated, but did not try to beg or grab. **Chris** explained that he had been training this dog. They had dog-sat this creature some while ago and when the owners were due to reclaim their pet their circumstances had changed and asked if **Chris** and **Beth** would look after him a while longer. Two years later they still are! When the food was nearing gone, the dog was getting ever more agitated, demonstrating what is normally the human fight between instinct and social conditioning. The dog duly got his tidbits.

DEC 31 Tessa supplies that learning

You might imagine that I wrote the words yesterday about that little plan to learn some more about Turkey was written as a postscript after my chat with **Tessa** today. We were talking about language acquisition when she said that in Turkey the children are exposed to multiple languages when young. How did she know I wanted to learn a little more about this country? Her family travel there try-annually, and she excitedly told about a former president who wanted to Westernise Turkey and actually changed their alphabet as part of this plan, giving it a Latin foundation.

On the way home I went to a Middle Eastern shop to buy some chillies. I asked a lady which were the strongest and which were not. She helped me out, and when she saw how little I was buying offered to give me one of hers. Said with a broad smile, by a lady from Gana, her generosity came from the heart. I declined but thanked her.

However, in spite of this cheery encounter, I think the combination of an endlessly crying baby in the coffee shop and the tedium and frustration of completing my tax return then triggered a very irritable state. Everything felt annoying!

Mid afternoon I decided I must go out to try to escape the irritability. I returned to Coffee #1 and pretty well instantly mellowed, probably because I decided that was how I wanted to be. I sat in a different seat than normal. One that afforded me a view of the counter on the very busy day. A mother sent her daughter scouting for seats and she looked forlorn. Since I was sat on one of five seats, I gave mine up. As I stood up, the girl looked at me. So exquisitely pretty. I correctly guessed that she was twelve. The mother was courteously grateful for the seats. I chatted merrily with the family in the conservatory.

And there endeth my diary of 2019 encounters.

Going back to earlier times

I will finish this book by going back to recount stories from my younger years. The earliest were from about 1979 to 1980, a consequence of my employment as a maintenance engineer at the BBC in London.

The first happened on day one of a temporary assignment away from the base of Broadcasting House to work at the Maida Vale studios where many sessions were recorded for Radio One and BBC TV in decades past. There was a pause in our work this day, a natural consequence of the fluctuating nature of repair work. So my boss said I could go to the main studio control room and sit in on a session being recorded. The pop group "The Police" were the other side of a double glazed window overlooking the studio itself. Two panes of glass with something like an eight inch gap between to deaden sound transmission.

They were recording a session for the John Peel show, including "Message in a bottle" that I particularly liked at the time. After a while, the band came into the control room, and I of course chatted with **Sting**. A stranger to me, but also not a stranger as I know him from afar. He was actually more shy than myself, which is rather odd for a 'brazen' musician. I eulogised about his music, and would now have cringed at how I must have come across.

My boss later got a bootleg copy of the reel-to-reel session. I had a reel-to-reel recorder and have that session on mini-disc now.

Another time, after watching my beloved Liverpool play at Spurs in the old division one, I printed some of the photographs I had taken and placed them in the studio in Broadcasting House that I knew John Peel would be broadcasting his 10pm programme from. I was on night shift at the time, and left the extension number of the engineers room. Later on he duly but kindly rang and invited me down for a chat.

Except that we talked at cross purposes for rather a while. He had thought the photos were from a European Cup fixture. But even so, not many people get to chat with a relatively private, but unique and amazing man. He even mentioned my name on air, and he curiously reminded me very much of my brother Ian.

When Peel entered the 'disk-jockeying' game, he felt rather like a fish out of water, and pretended on air to be talking to his mate to ease his nerves. The intimacy this created became his style. He also was a madly keen Liverpool fan, even marrying in an all red suit.

The final story from this time of my life saw me visit the Broadcasting House newsroom. Not an easy place to fix machines as the staff were, let me say, rather blunt and unhelpful, presumably always too busy on some intense and urgent news item. This time, I was working alone fixing a Studer reel to reel recorder. About the size and shape of a gas cooker.

As I worked away, a powerfully built man appeared with a white suited man as accompaniment. He was greeted by news staff who talked with him. But after a while, he peeled away and came over to me to shake my hand. My hand was swallowed inside his.

It was **Mohamed Ali**.

That he would make a point of leaving famous people to embrace a humble worker shows the nature of the man. I was necessarily moved by his gesture and have repeated this story countless times.

I found the photograph taken that day by one on the newsroom staff, with Ali in the foreground, and my head peaking out from behind the second person from the left.

In the 1990's, I played tennis with a passion in Portsmouth on the South Coast of England where I lived in the employment of IBM as a systems and then applications programmer. For a town so bombarded by wind that the trees alongside the sea-front tennis courts were bedecked with branches and leaves on one side only, tennis was crazily popular. Fortunately, a Navy built indoor tennis 'bubble' with four courts supplied many years of respite from the elements.

On one occasion, I was explaining to a fellow social-tennis-night player that I was able to go to a Grammar school in 1968 without the need to pass the 11-plus exam. Originally this was the filtering method chosen to select the 'cream' of young people to give 'superior' teaching to. At least that was the principle.

It was Bishopshalt Grammar School in West London, a most beautiful building with magnificent grounds that I had to leave behind almost as soon as I joined, my family emigrating to Wales in 1969.

The lady I was regaling this story to explained that she actually did sit the 11-plus exam, but her headteacher did not like her, and contrived to 'lose' her paper, somehow. I never fully worked out why it was not found or why she was not allowed to resit it. The curious matter is that her presumed ability to pass the 11-plus and attend a grammar school, but be denied, was the opposite of my position. And it was the very same London school she had been hoping to attend, as this was where she lived at the time.

Most curious!

A few years ago, maybe as many as ten, I got involved in a chat with a poorly blighted man as we sat by the bowling green at my tennis club. This unfortunate fellow had terminal cancer, but rose above that plight to engage in good spirit with me. The conversation lurched from one subject to another until it alighted on nutrition for vegetarians.

I mentioned that *quorn* was now a well accepted source of protein in modern vegetarian diets, allowing meat substitutes of surprisingly good taste and texture to be made. In the 1970's, this man proceeded to explain that he was on the development team for a myco-protein, made from mushrooms that was marketed as quorn.

On holiday in Austria some years ago, I caught the coach to Salzburg, and eagerly sought out the parts where "The Sound of Music" was filmed. The steps where I believed they sang 'Doh ray me' seemed too few in number. So

I asked a family walking past if I was indeed in the right place. They confirmed and even let me join them for lunch where I learnt that they had travelled to America to visit the place that the original Maria the film revolved around had lived. I think they might even have met her.

More recently, I was chatting to a man in The Retreat pub on the Llanedeyrn estate in Cardiff. I told him that my family had moved into the Pennsylvania area of that estate at the time of its construction in 1970 I believe it was. We only stayed a year or two. To which he declared that he had moved into the adjacent Chapel Wood area not long afterwards. Some years later, they relocated and moved to Pennsylvania.

To number 74 Pennsylvania.

The very house we had lived in.

The author on Penarth Pier

A few tips for talking with strangers

 Do not fear talking to people you do not know. Just start by saying hello or commenting on their appearance or even the weather.

 Speak with an upbeat tone to put others at ease. This can make it easier for strangers to respond and open out to you.

 Talk with people in supermarket queues, at bus stops, on the bus, in the coffee shop, while out walking, at the tennis club ... wherever you go, you can find people to connect with, even if for just a few seconds. Often a moment just long enough to receive a smile.

 Do not judge strangers on how they look. Let feelings of the unknown or difference fade away so that you too can open out to them. Accepting them as they are makes chat easier and lighter. When they sense they are being accepted unconditionally, they will likely relax and open out. You can even make a point of saying hello to people you do not like the look of. This can often dissolve the bias in your mind that makes you feel uncomfortable. That in turn can then make you more open to all that you meet, less likely to pre-judge.

 Allow people to reject you! Some are busy, some are having a bad day, some prefer not to talk to strangers. Some will even give you a dirty look. Accept that rejection can occasionally happen and do not emotionally react. Let ill feelings fade and move on. You will, however, find that most people most of the time are happy to connect, even if just briefly.

 In conversation, ask about the other person, their interests, their job. Try to feel their life, even if alien to you own. Explore and learn from what they say. Try not to compete, though. Try to keep the chat a dialogue rather than a monologue in either direction.

 If the conversation becomes confrontational, try to ease back from your own viewpoint to see theirs. You can learn a great deal when you challenge your own perspectives. But if they continue to attack rather than inform, then it is best to escape politely from the chat.

Printed in Great Britain
by Amazon

79496774R00099